Surviving Technopolis

Surviving Technopolis

Essays on Finding Balance
in Our New Man-Made Environments

Arthur W. Hunt III

Foreword by
Anthony Selvaggio

PICKWICK *Publications* · Eugene, Oregon

SURVIVING TECHNOPOLIS
Essays on Finding Balance in Our New Man-made Environments

Pickwick Publications
An Imprint of Wipf and Stock Publishers
199 W. 8th Ave., Suite 3
Eugene, OR 97401

www.wipfandstock.com

ISBN 13: 978-1-62032-714-2

Cataloguing-in-Publication data:

Hunt, Arthur W., 1960–.

Surviving technopolis : essays on finding balance in our new man-made environments / Arthur W. Hunt III ; foreword by Anthony Selvaggio.

xvi + 254 pp. ; 23 cm. Includes bibliographical references.

ISBN 13: 978-1-62032-714-2

1. Digital media and culture. 2. Technology—Social aspects. 3. Technology assessment. I. Selvaggio, Anthony. II. Title.

T14.5 .H77 2013

This book is dedicated to my father
Arthur W. Hunt, Jr.

The Great Depression was a miserable period, yet he spoke of it as the happiest time of his life. Devoted family members, garden plots, fishing holes, and affectionate neighbors fill his memories.

Contents

Foreword

Anthony Selvaggio

I FIRST MET ARTHUR Hunt when I was the Pastor of the College Hill Reformed Presbyterian Church in Beaver Falls, Pennsylvania. Art had come to town to teach in the communications department at Geneva College, which was across the street from the church. Art decided to attend our church and we shared many opportunities to talk about various issues from Reformed theology to Media Ecology. When those conversations began, I had no idea what Media Ecology was.

Over the course of the next two years, Art became a Presbyterian, and I became convinced of the importance of Media Ecology, particularly to developing and maintaining a Christian worldview. I believe I played only a small role in Art's transition to Reformed theology (he was already heading in that direction), but he played a major role in shaping my understanding of Media Ecology. In God's providence, during this time Art and I also had the privilege of being near Dr. T. David Gordon of Grove City College, another Christian who has done serious studies in the area of Media Ecology and its application to the Christian mind. This was a rich intellectual time for me, a time for which I will always be grateful.

Art and I found kinship over many ideas, foremost of which was our mutual desire to contemplate, cultivate and preserve what T. S. Eliot referred to as the "permanent things." My interactions with Art clearly influenced my book, *7 Toxic Ideas Polluting Your Mind* (P&R Publishing, 2011), which deals with the erosion of the Christian mind in our age and draws upon the insights of Media Ecology. I am indebted to Art for how his thoughts have enriched my own.

Now I have the pleasure of having Art further enrich my mind and thoughts through this book. I believe your mind will also be enriched because the reader will find in these pages a full-orbed and mature exploration of the symptoms of modern life that are eroding our lives, minds and souls. But Art is not content with simply diagnosing the problem; instead he provides a framework for addressing the problem. He shows us a path back to a simpler, richer, and fuller life. In showing us this path, Art is not simply pining for a world that was, but rather he points us forward to a world that can be—a world of *telos*. Ultimately, this type of world is not realized geographically as a spot on a map, but rather eschatologically as a state of heart and mind. Art points us to a world that can only be fully realized in the consummation of our Lord, but he beckons us to experience, in the here and now, a foretaste of that glorious future by calling us to apply its principles wherever we find ourselves. In this book, Art sets before us a world that is worth proclaiming, protecting and preserving. A world that Tolkien's hobbits affectionately referred to as "the Shire."

Acknowledgments

SPECIAL APPRECIATION IS EXTENDED to Anthony Selvaggio, who, when I complained about Walmart one day, suggested I read Wendell Berry; to Eric Miller who perceived I was deeply troubled when he saw me in the Geneva College library with an armload of books that signaled the loss of community life; to Ralph Ancil for quality hours of conversation on Richard Weaver and others who have declared, "I'll Take My Stand"; to Lance Strate and Corey Anton who are the very models of modern media ecologists; to Robert Nanney and Jerald Ogg who have encouraged me in my research efforts; to my fellow hobbits at the University of Tennessee at Martin: Christopher Brown, John Schommer, Nathan Howard, John Glass, Sam Richardson, Norman Lillegard, Father Dennis Schenkel, Bob Peckham, and Chris Hill; to those who read and remarked on my manuscript: Read Schuchardt, T. David Gordon, Carl Trueman, Justin Barnard, Mary Beard, and Charlie Collier; and finally, to my affectionate family who must know by now that my concern over the issues raised in this book is no passing fancy.

Introduction

Meet George Jetson

Jane, stop this crazy thing!
—GEORGE JETSON

POOR GEORGE JETSON.

He works three hours a day, three days a week, pushing a single button. He has a loving family. He drives a flying car. But he cannot manage the automatic walking machine.

If you grew up in the 1960s as I did, *The Jetsons* was top Saturday morning cartoon fare. As I remember it, the show opens with jazzy music as the Jetson family darts across the sky in their bubbled rocketmobile.

"Meet George Jetson . . . his boy Elroy . . . daughter Judy . . . Jane, his wife."

The close of the show is less cheery, but just as amusing. George arrives home and is greeted by Rosie the housekeeping robot. George reclines in his conveyor chair and scoots around to Elroy who pops on his slippers. Judy plops on a kiss. Jane hands him dog Astro for the evening stroll. But when the cat jumps on the treadmill all control is lost. All George can do is scream his head off as his body rotates round and round outside the Skypad apartments.

"Jane, stop this crazy thing!"

The cleverness of *The Jetsons* cartoon was showing the wondrous possibilities associated with a bright technological future and then contrasting that with unforeseeable misfortune.

Everything is automated, but the Jetsons eat pills for dinner.

Cars fly in the skyway, but the birds have taken to walking on the ground.

Rosie the robot is a good ol' girl, but she can turn on you.

I cannot help but think that more and more people are having those George Jetson moments where they want to cry, "Stop the world, I want to get off!" What I am talking about is a gut feeling that something is very, very wrong—a sense of powerlessness and despair.

For me, these feelings come at the oddest times. Sometimes they come when I am sitting in a traffic jam, and I want to strangle the steering wheel because I know a person should not travel an hour-and-a-half to work in a car. Then I get to work and turn on my computer, and there are five hundred emails waiting for me. Do I even know five hundred people? (It is my understanding that Bill Gates used to get four million pieces of email per day, a fact I find strangely gratifying.) When I saw the Twin Towers falling down, I knew something was awfully wrong with the world. It wasn't just that terrorists attacked us, but that for days the television kept showing the collapsing buildings over and over and over. Then there was the TV reporter covering the invasion of Iraq who screamed like he was calling an NFL football game: "Shock and awe! Shock and awe!" A feeling of dread came upon me when I first learned the top of my house could be viewed by anyone who had a personal computer. Then there was Al Gore standing there with his PowerPoint presentation, telling me the earth has a fever. The earth has a fever? The world used to be so big; now we talk about it as if it were a sick child. Not too long ago I was discussing with my students how scientists had recently implanted silicon chips in the brains of monkeys. The experiment allowed the animals to interact with a computer without touching the mouse. One student gushed over its practical implications—not for monkeys, but for human beings. When I asked him if he would buy such a device for his own brain he responded without hesitation, "Absolutely." "And would you buy a chip for your brain that would allow you to watch videos any time you like?" "Absolutely," he said.

"Jane, stop this crazy thing!"

I am not one to put too much stock in gut feelings, but I have come to the conclusion that something has gone wrong with the world. The problem of which I speak goes beyond the acknowledgment of evil or what theologians call original sin. As a Calvinist, I certainly believe that evil exists and that sin resides in us all. What these essays address, however, is that the world is qualitatively different than it was one hundred or two hundred years ago, not only technologically but also economically, psychologically and spiritually. In regard to magnitude, force, and speed, the nature of our predicament has no precedent. For purposes here we will simply call it *Technopolis*.

Other names have been used for the condition to which I am referring.

Historian and philosopher of technology Lewis Mumford preferred the term *megamachine* by which he meant an *irrational drive toward profit and power*. The megamachine, Mumford insisted, brings us deepening alienation, dehumanization, war, environmental destruction, and possible annihilation.

French sociologist and theologian Jacques Ellul employed the term *La Technique* to describe our *abdication of moral discourse for technological know-how*. Ellul said the pursuit of technical efficiency muffles moral discourse in the public arena and ultimately contributes to the dehumanization of society.

Media theorist and cultural critic Neil Postman used the term *Technopoly*, a condition in which *all forms of cultural life have surrendered to the sovereignty of technology*. Postman said the American culture engaged in a great Faustian bargain whereby it exchanged old ideas and tradition for the promises offered through technological fulfillment.

Christian author and apologist C. S. Lewis would have agreed with much of the analysis offered by Mumford, Ellul, and Postman regarding technological society. Lewis certainly had an opinion about where practical science was taking us as articulated in his classic work *The Abolition of Man*. Lewis spoke of *man's conquest of nature becoming nature's conquest of man*. Lewis warned us how powerful technologies beyond human scale, plus the absence of traditional and universal morality (the Tao), plus the willingness of some to use these technologies over the many, could produce the demise of man.

Whether we call it the *megamachine, La Technique, Technopoly*, or the *Abolition of Man*, makes little difference. These labels are all getting at the same thing. To boil it down, Technopolis refers to our new manmade environments—now gone global—and how they intentionally and unintentionally alter the economic, social, and moral fabric of our lives. In this sense Technopolis is not just about new and powerful technologies; it is about the technological milieu in which we swim. Ultimately, these essays address the subject of what people are for—that is, the implications of being created in God's image. Unfortunately, Technopolis has no end in view other than bigger, faster, newer, and more. And while giving us many material benefits (at least in the short run), in its wake are spiritual loss, alienation, and natural devastation.

These essays not only evaluate Technopolis, but also seek wisdom to cope with our new man-made environments. Positively stated, they offer suggestions on how to bring us back into balance. Some of our best wisdom in analyzing Technopolis can be found in voices of the Christian humanists. Unlike Enlightenment humanism, which tends to be man-centered, Christian humanism is concerned with the role of humankind within God's created order. G. K. Chesterton, T. S. Eliot, J. R. R. Tolkien, and C. S. Lewis represent this tradition. They, and others like them, understood that technological progress with no clear *telos* obscures what Eliot called "the permanent things."

1

Remembering Marshall McLuhan

The Probes of the Media Guru
Are Still Relevant for Us Today

*Unlike previous environmental changes, the electric media constitute a
total near instantaneous transformation of culture, values, and attitudes.*

—MARSHALL MCLUHAN[1]

SHORTLY AFTER PUBLISHING *UNDERSTANDING Media* in 1964, Marshall
McLuhan appeared before a New York audience and casually predicted
the invention of the iPhone headset: "There might come a day when we
[will] . . . all have portable computers, about the size of a hearing aid, to help
us mesh our personal experience with the experience of the great wired
brain of the outer world."[2] The great wired world of which he spoke came
to be more commonly referred to as the global village, a term he coined,
and by which he meant *electronic interdependence.* McLuhan anticipated
that all electronic media, taken together, would restructure the world as
we know it. Information would flow instantaneously from one situation to
another, from every quarter of the earth, so that the globe would become a
small village-like affair. In this new environment, whatever happens to any-
body happens to everybody.[3] He saw it as the externalization of the human
subconscious on a global scale, and it was coming together in his lifetime.

1. McLuhan and Zingrone, *Essential McLuhan*, 238–39.
2. Marchand, *Marshall McLuhan*, 180.
3. Molinaro, et al., *Letters of Marshall McLuhan*, 253.

He said soon the "new society will be one mythic integration, a resonating world akin to the old tribal echo chamber where magic will live again; a world of ESP."[4] The year 2011 marked the media guru's one-hundredth birthday. Had he not died in 1980, he no doubt would be on Oprah today saying, "I told you this was coming."

McLuhan believed the only way to survive a world predicated on constant change was to stand back and scrutinize its patterns. His methodology was a matter of *seeing*, and he compared what he was doing to Edgar Allen Poe's "A Descent into the Maelstrom." In Poe's story a sailor is caught in the tentacles of a swirling vortex. While pondering his fate, the sailor notices how some objects remained at the surface and were not affected by the current. The sailor secures himself to a barrel, abandons his boat, and saves himself from drowning.

Like the sailor in Poe's story we also must learn to stand outside the remarkable forces that swirl around us and ponder their effects. Only then can we keep ourselves from being sucked down into an electronic vortex. McLuhan liked to call his observations "probes"—announcements and predictions about pattern change that often went unnoticed by society at large—unnoticed because moderns tend to embrace all technological change without thinking very hard about its unintended consequences. Those who are already familiar with McLuhan are still deciphering the profundity of these probes. Others are amazed at how he shrewdly anticipated the arrival of the global village. McLuhan's probes are just important today as they were when he first pronounced them—more important really—because our attention spans have not gotten any longer.

Marshall McLuhan, What Were You Doin'?

McLuhan was born into a Protestant family but converted to Catholicism as a young man. He would have been content to have been born during the Middle Ages, but providence placed him in the twentieth century where he became an astute observer of change. He earned his PhD from the University of Cambridge, fashioning himself as a literary scholar. The rejection of his religious heritage (he was raised Baptist) was due in part to his disappointment with what he thought Protestant culture had produced. He was influenced early-on by Old World Catholic G. K. Chesterton whose sharp pen criticized the Protestant tendency to embrace all things new in

4. McLuhan and Zingrone, *Essential McLuhan*, 261.

the name of "progress." By the time he reached Cambridge he confessed to his mother that everything that was "especially hateful and devilish and inhuman about the conditions and strains of modern industrial society is not only Protestant in origin, but their boast (!) to have originated it."[5] McLuhan was appalled at American utilitarianism. "The Americans serve 'service,'" he wrote to his mother. "Like the rest of the world they have smothered man and men and set up the means as the end."[6]

Although Canadian born, his first teaching positions were in America where he soon realized that his students were more influenced by advertising, comic books, and movies than anything he might offer in the way of Dickens or Hawthorne. The divide between his world and theirs astonished him, so he took it upon himself to infuse popular culture into the subjects he taught, the goal being to make his students grasp the type of influence he thought the commercial world was exerting over them.

Not everyone saw what McLuhan saw. After the publishing of *The Gutenberg Galaxy* in 1962, and *Understanding Media* two years later, he threw down a public gauntlet saying electronic communication would undo the old print society. Heads started to turn. His meteoric rise was due in part to his uncanny ability to deliver mouth-dropping one-liners. He said things like Blondie was emasculating Dagwood in front of Cookie and Alexander— proof the American male had been reduced to a shell.[7] He told *Playboy* magazine in 1969 that the day of political democracy was over. He said peculiar things like, "The Finn cycle of tribal institutions can return in the electric age, but if again, then let's make it a wake or awake or both."[8] (This particular quotation alludes to James Joyce's *Finnegans Wake*, a work McLuhan embraced as paralleling his own understanding of human communication and its cyclical view of history.) Statements like these made him a charlatan to some and a genius to others. Henry Gibson of *Laugh-In* looked into the television camera and asked, "Marshall McLuhan, what are you doin'?"

Early in his career McLuhan was unafraid to make moral pronouncements, but as his star shot above the cultural horizon he was more reluctant to comment on the "goodness" or "badness" of what he was talking about. Anyone who reads *The Mechanical Bride* (1951) can sense a certain animosity toward the ravishing power of industrialism and its chief agent,

5. Quoted in Molinaro, et al., *Letters of Marshall McLuhan*, 73.
6. Ibid., 74.
7. See Gordon, *Marshall McLuhan*, 98.
8. McLuhan, *Medium is the Massage*, 120.

modern advertising. Interestingly, he would not let his own children watch more than one hour of television per week.[9] One of his biographers says that his study of media was almost an act of revenge for what it was doing to his family, to him, and the world.[10] As a result, he developed a personae that made him appear to be above the cultural convulsions that were occurring with the new media. Hence he became a self-proclaimed observer, detached from his subject. He had learned from James Joyce that oracles are not supposed to take sides.[11]

In reviewing *Understanding Media* Harold Rosenberg remarked, "In his latest mood, he [McLuhan] regards most of what is going on today as highly desirable, all of it meaningful."[12] In his interview with *Playboy* McLuhan said that until he had written *The Mechanical Bride*, he had adopted an "extremely moralistic approach to all environmental technology,"[13] and then added that he was not "advocating anything." "I am merely probing and predicting trends. Even if I opposed them or thought them disastrous, I couldn't stop them, so why waste my time lamenting?"[14]

Since McLuhan was underscoring the importance of the new electronic media, television gladly embraced him. He rubbed shoulders with the corporate world, advising businesses on the media they sought to harness. But perhaps more than anything, his popularity was due to the fact he was offering answers—even if they were off-the-wall answers—during turbulent times when political assassinations, campus riots, and a sexual revolution were making headlines. Journalists elevated him to the status of a sage, calling him everything from "media guru" to "oracle of the electronic age." More recently, *Wired Magazine* made him its "patron saint."

McLuhan was boldly unconventional.[15] He never really made "scientific claims" about anything. He preferred to toss his probes like grenades. He did not *persuade* his audience; he simply *declared* his point of view even if it left those around him baffled. He brazenly used fuzzy terminology. His best known phrases, McLuhanisms as they came to be called, included

9. Marchand, *Marshall McLuhan*, 69.

10. Ibid., 158.

11. Ibid., 218.

12. Ibid., 179.

13. McLuhan and Zingrone, *Essential McLuhan*, 265–66.

14. Ibid., 264.

15. See Meyrowitz, "Canonic," 191–94, for McLuhan's methodology and style of discourse elaborated here.

"hot" and "cool" media, "the medium is the message," and of course "the global village." As if he knew his time capsule would one day be opened by a new species of man unaccustomed to reading words on a page, he deliberately avoided traditional linear logic and instead used a more elliptical style of discourse loaded with metaphors and puns.

McLuhan was capable of writing superb literary criticism and he did so in his early career, but as he became more popular, he had a difficult time sitting still and would rather have his editors "fix" his erratic prose. He preferred talking anyway and enjoyed nothing more than to gather his students together for an evening of "probing." He loathed academic specialization and considered himself a generalist. Neil Postman said of him, "He was the first writer I had ever encountered who could write a sentence in which the words Plato, Erasmus, Batman, and the Beatles could find a coherent place."[16] Academia had a hard time swallowing his pronouncements. Either a lack of comprehension, or doubt, or sheer jealousy prevented his inclusion into their fragmented circles of knowledge. McLuhan refused to occupy himself with one little scholarly nook as they did. He was determined to connect all the dots.

Retribalized Man

Marshall McLuhan—to rephrase Henry Gibson's question—"What *were* you doin'?" The Canadian communication theorist held that all media, regardless of the messages they communicate, dramatically influence man and society. We shape our technologies, and in turn they shape us. He asserted that all technological innovations are extensions of our bodies. For example, the fork is an extension of the hand, the chair is an extension of the spine, gloves are an extension of the skin, and so forth. Each extension enhances the ability and the sense, sometimes to the determent of other abilities and senses. Forks and chairs are rather simple amplifications, but powerful technologies can be radically transforming. For the longest time tribal man existed in harmonious balance with the five senses: hearing, touch, smell, sight, and taste. But then humans began to make things that disrupted this balance.

McLuhan postulated that there had been three major technological innovations in human communication that had dramatically reshaped society. First, the phonetic alphabet jolted tribal man to eye dominance.

16. See Postman, Foreword to *Marshall McLuhan*, x.

Second, movable type further accelerated the eye dominance. Finally, the electronics revolution began the process of retribalizing man and restoring his sensory balance. When McLuhan spoke of *tribal man* he meant pre-literate man when humans lived close together and communicated orally. Because there was no formal writing system, the primary modes of communication for pre-literate man were sight and sound.

When the phonetic alphabet came along, it broke-up the tribal circle. The eye was extended and the ear was suppressed. In-depth communal interplay was replaced with visual linear values and segmented consciousness.[17] The alphabet created societies that were characteristically fragmented, individualistic, explicit, logical, specialized, and detached.[18] The Greeks experimented with democracy, and the Romans created bureaucracies because writing allowed these cultures to order experience uniformly and sequentially. Visual man extended his eye via the alphabet to see the terrain beyond where he stood so he could control, exploit, or conquer it. Knowledge applied was the power to organize and mobilize, to accelerate action and alter forms.[19]

McLuhan remarked that while the phonetic alphabet was like a bombshell falling on tribal man, the printing press was like a one-hundred-megaton H-bomb.[20] The printing press radically altered Europe and eventually the world with its capacity to reproduce information in unlimited quantities and at much faster speeds. The printing press also had the effect of reducing generalists. Or, as McLuhan would say, the Renaissance destroyed Renaissance man. Print technology brought about a general explosion in knowledge giving rise to the scientist, putting to death the enchanter. "The invention of typography," says McLuhan, "confirmed and extended the new visual stress of applied knowledge, providing the first uniformly repeatable commodity, the first assembly-line, and the first mass production."[21] While the phonetic alphabet gave power to organize, mobilize, accelerate action, and alter forms, the printing press gave out this power on a grand scale.

One of McLuhan's observations about media is that they can reverse the effects they create. The printing press gave rise to industrialism, which ironically gave rise to the new electronic culture, which shares

17. McLuhan and Zingrone, *Essential McLuhan*, 240.

18. Ibid.

19. Ibid., 242.

20. Ibid., 243.

21. McLuhan, *Gutenberg Galaxy*, 153.

characteristics with primitive oral cultures. Electronic media act to reverse the effects of print media, creating environments antithetical to the modern era. Print is an extension of the eye, but the new electronic media are an extension of the nervous system—the externalization of the human subconscious on a global scale. "Now man is beginning to wear his brain outside his skull and his nerves outside his skin," he said, "new technology breeds new man."[22] McLuhan called this new creature "discarnate man," a person who routinely invites a wide assortment of humanity into his living room via television; a person who can be present anywhere in the world, absent his body. The new electronic environment retribalizes man by placing him in a new acoustic space. Just as conventional tribal civilizations are often deprived of private and personal morality, so are members of the electronic tribe. Everyone is known by everyone. The transformational power of the emerging global village is nearly total as it obliterates old social taboos and transforms political institutions.

As early as 1960 McLuhan was making statements about the tribal nature of contemporary adolescents. The Sexual Revolution had not yet reached a boiling point, but he was already talking about how teenagers conformed to tribal mores, performed tribal rituals, and suppressed individuality.[23] "Our teenage generation is already becoming part of a jungle clan," he said. "As youth enters this clan world and all their senses are electronically extended and intensified, there is a corresponding amplification of their sexual sensibilities . . ."[24] If McLuhan were alive today he would have no doubt explained the popularity of tattoos and body piercing as a reverting back to tribal modes of expression. Likewise, the general rise of sexual promiscuity within the culture and the willingness for young people to expose themselves electronically, literally or otherwise, McLuhan would say, is a reverting back to tribal modes of expression.

McLuhan's prognoses about political affairs were just as jolting as his musings about the sexual mores of young people. He predicted that John F. Kennedy would win the 1960 election over Richard Nixon after seeing them debate on television. Nixon projected an image of "the railway lawyer who signs leases that are not in the best interests of the folks in the little town." "If he would even grow sideburns," he later said, people would change their

---

22. McLuhan and Zingrone, *Essential McLuhan*, 264–65.
23. Marchand, *Marshall McLuhan*, 157.
24. McLuhan and Zingrone, *Essential McLuhan*, 252.

attitudes toward him.[25] On the other hand, Kennedy came across as "the shy young sheriff." Kennedy's "cool" personality was better suited for television, a cool medium that was low in sensory participation, one level up from casual conversation, where the receiver fills in the missing data with her own perception.

McLuhan insisted that a politician's image was more important than his actual person. In the future the politician would be more of a tribal chieftain than a representative of any particular party: "The new politician showman has to literally as well as figuratively put on his audience as he would a suit of clothes and become a corporate tribal image—like Mussolini, Hitler and F.D.R. . . . All these men were tribal emperors on a scale theretofore unknown in the world, because they mastered their media."[26]

The figure of the new tribal chieftain would reciprocate a new political order where traditional voting would no longer be needed. McLuhan believed that polls and projections had already made the old electoral process obsolete. He asserted that the day of the super state was over, not only for the United States, but for the rest of the world because the planet was connecting-up into a single tribe where speech, drum, and ear would live again through everywhere-at-once technologies. World events would echo daily from the tribal drum. Indeed, the everywhere media have borne this out. "Princess Di was killed today in a terrible automobile accident." Boom. Boom. Boom. "I did not have relations with that woman, Monica Lewinsky." Boom. Boom. Boom. "Osama bin Laden was shot in the head today." Boom. Boom. Boom.

McLuhan was concerned we would not be able to cope with the speed and magnitude of change wrought by the new electronic environments. The swirling vortex of change would threaten old identities to such a degree that people—even entire nations—would violently lash out to retrieve what they once were. "When our identity is in danger, we feel certain that we have a mandate for war. The old image must be recovered at any cost." There is little doubt that McLuhan would have interpreted the attack on the Twin Towers as a calculated back fist against what some perceived as decadence, a kind of corruption that was oozing into the crevasses of the Islamic world, even if it was coming to them under the pretext of "freedom" and "markets." Images of Madonna and Michael Jackson are declarations

25. See Marchand, *Marshall McLuhan*, 160–61, for McLuhan's views on the Nixon-Kennedy televised debate.

26. McLuhan and Zingrone, *Essential McLuhan*, 247.

of war to the Islamic fundamentalist who knows his culture is threatened by their iconic all-encompassing presence. "I can't study anymore," complained one Islamic youth. "I have become impatient, weak and nervous. I feel crippled . . . so vulgar and stimulating [are those images]."[27]

McLuhan contemplated how the global village and its mythic consciousness could usher back the gods and goddesses of ancient antiquity, or as Camille Paglia, an admirer of McLuhan put it, "Popular culture is the new Babylon, into which so much art and intellect now flow. It is our imperial sex theater, supreme temple of the western eye. We live in the age of idols. The pagan past, never dead, flames again in our mystic hierarchies of stardom."[28] The global village, despite its touted economic benefits, operates as a culture of spectacle. It is the tribal fire everyone squats around.

Christ or Chaos?

Although McLuhan's writings have been criticized for being obscure, and although his speaking performances sometimes left audiences scratching their heads, when one stands back and surveys his entire work, an overarching narrative comes into view. Neil Postman, who considered himself an intellectual child of McLuhan, says that McLuhan's story is one of both loss and redemption.[29] More specifically, it is one that is reminiscent of the biblical narrative of Paradise, Expulsion, and Paradise Regained. *Paradise* because in the beginning human communication was what it was intended to be—oral, holistic, and full-bodied with all the senses harmoniously balanced. *Expulsion* because the balance was upset as man extended himself through his technologies and fragmented his sensorium. The phonetic alphabet was especially upsetting, as was the printing press, the later ushering in the modern age with its compartmental, ultra-rational, and ultimately secular worldview. *Paradise Regained* because electronic communication was bringing the sensorium back into balance.

It should be pointed out that such a storyline does not parallel the biblical narrative of Creation, Fall, and Redemption. Nevertheless, McLuhan perceived history as a kind of loop: tribe to anti-tribe to electronic tribe. The electronic tribe is wrought with dangers to be sure, but McLuhan also saw

27. Peter Waldman, "Iran Fights New Foe: Western Television," Wall Street Journal, August 8, 1994, A10, as quoted in Barber, *Jihad*, 314.

28. Paglia, *Sexual Personae*, 139.

29. Postman, Foreword to *Marshall McLuhan*, ix.

potential in it as well. It was an optimism permitted in his evolving Catholicism, and perhaps more than anything else, his own take on the theology of Pierre Teilhard de Chardin that made him suggest that the "psychic communal integration" made possible by electronic media could create a universal consciousness assumed in the future mystical body of Christ.[30]

While the public McLuhan could appear optimistic about where the new media were heading, there was always the pessimistic McLuhan lurking in the shadows. He had said things could go either way—Christ or chaos: "The extensions of man's consciousness induced by the electric media could conceivably usher in the millennium, but it also holds the potential for realizing the Anti-Christ—Yeat's rough beast, its hour come round at last, . . . slouching toward Bethlehem to be born."[31] Toward the end of his life he contemplated again the possibilities of apocalypse. The more he thought about it, the more he saw how the global village presented itself as a "world between fantasy and dream" where the self would be swallowed up in a world of images.[32] The destruction of our private identities produced the unpleasant consequence of fostering children incapable of civilized pursuits: "I myself think they are sinking into a kind of world where satisfactions are pathetically crude and feeble, compared to the ones we took for granted thirty years ago. . . . Their kicks are on a seven-or eight-year-old level."[33] He complained that children raised on television seem "aimless, undisciplined, and illiterate."[34]

It would be easy to fault McLuhan for his ambiguity on whether the global village would turn out to be a shining city on a hill or go up in flames. After all, he was the one who coined the term, and you would think he would have been more certain of its outcome. But before we cast stones we should remember that the vast majority of Christians also have not made up their minds about the merit of our new global village. Even those whose eschatology requires an apocalypse seem to embrace the great electronic hook-up on economic grounds. While deriding big government (justifiably so) Christian "conservatives" are quick to defend the creation of the global village and all that it entails—the expansion of global corporate power at the expense of suppressing smaller entities like the traditional family and

30. Marchand, *Marshall McLuhan*, 216.

31. McLuhan and Zingrone, *Essential McLuhan*, 268.

32. See Marchand, *Marshall McLuhan*, 249.

33. Ibid.

34. Ibid.

local communities. Screen-time hours for Christians vary little from non-Christians. We watch the same shows, have the same patterns of spending, and go into debt like everyone else. Most of us are card-carrying members in the culture of consumption. At least McLuhan put the brakes on his own children's media habits.

McLuhan was reflecting his Old World sensibilities in expressing doubts about the possibility of the global village shoring up a mystical body of Christ. After all, to suggest that Christ will come to commune with his church via the World Wide Web seems a bit out of sync with revealed religion, and possibly confuses the Holy Spirit with electricity. Moreover, it should be said that time spent in the virtual world decreases time spent in the real one, and this is crucial because the real world is where people develop a sense of identity in relationship to others and in relationship to a geographical space that places limits on them. As Wendell Berry reminds us, "There can be no such thing as a 'global village.' No matter how much one may love the world as a whole, one can live fully in it only by living responsibly in some small part of it."[35] Substituting the virtual world for the real one is like mistaking a map for the land itself. The computer allows the soul to be anywhere at any time for any reason, but it does not privilege the body in this way. The ability to disembody oneself, to send it out through electronic channels that have been created for often ambiguous motives, unsettles the theological notion that humans were purposed as unified creatures, soul and body joined together. Up until the invention of the telegraph, and its successor the personal computer, humans had never experienced the kind of disembodiment now associated with the computer age.

McLuhan is worth remembering because he saw the necessity of standing back and observing the patterns of change that swirl around us. Instead of uncritically embracing every new technology that comes along, we should keep in mind his most important probe: that we shape our technologies, and in turn they shape us.

35. Berry, *Unsettling of America*, 123.

2

Neil Postman and the Evangelicals

He was basically a secular Jew, and I am basically a conservative
Christian, but he taught me more than almost any Christian I can
think of (C. S. Lewis?).[1]

—DR. T. DAVID GORDON

DR. GORDON'S COMMENT, WHICH appeared in an online post among other
recollections of Neil Postman, demonstrates how well the media theorist
and educator, who passed away in October 2003, is held in high regard
by a selection of evangelical academics and scholars. To rank Postman up
there with the author and apologist C. S. Lewis is no small matter for a
Christian educator like Gordon who teaches Greek and Religion at Grove
City College in western Pennsylvania. This is not to say that the entire evangelical community is familiar with Postman or would agree with the basic
thrust of his writings, for evangelicalism is a big pond with an assortment
of diverse fish, many paying no attention whatsoever to the water in which
they swim. It would be more accurate to say that it is a particular kind of
evangelical fish that likes to quote Postman—a reflective fish, a Reformed
fish, a confessional fish, a fish out of water.

This essay attempts to explain why certain evangelicals consider Postman, if not their favorite teacher, at least one of their favorite teachers, despite never having sat in a classroom with him or ever hearing of something
called the New York School. First, a definition of evangelicalism is in order,
coupled with a description of the sort of evangelical that affectionately

1. Gordon, "Neil Postman," n.p.

leans upon Postman. Second, Postman's philosophical outlook is compared and contrasted with these evangelicals to ascertain the intersecting lines of agreement relating to a critical assessment of American culture. Finally, some samples of evangelical scholarship that relies heavily on Postman's work are reviewed.

What Is an Evangelical Anyway?

According to a Gallup survey, roughly four out of ten Americans identify themselves as evangelical or born-again Christians.[2] Billy Graham, whose ministry began in the 1940s with citywide crusades, is often regarded as the elder statesman of modern American evangelicalism. But one must go back to the 1740s and the preaching of Jonathan Edwards and George Whitefield to understand the beginnings of a movement that shook both America and Great Britain. The Great Awakening was in essence a "re-statement of the older Puritan teaching on the need for men first to be humbled if they are to be soundly converted."[3] "New-Lights" like Edwards claimed that true religion goes beyond human reason to touch the affections. Edwards believed a personal relationship with God wrought by a conversion experience was in keeping with the spirit of the Reformation as articulated by Martin Luther and John Calvin. Wheaton College historian Mark Noll says that from the beginning evangelicalism emphasized spiritual renewal over ecclesiastical formalism and made a popular appeal for living a "religion of the heart."[4] British historian David Bebbington identifies four common elements within evangelicalism: conversionism (an emphasis on the new birth as a life-changing experience), biblicism (recognizing the Bible as ultimate authority in religious matters), activism (the sharing of faith), and crucicentrism (a focus on the redeeming work of Christ as the sole way of salvation).[5]

Although the Great Awakening was felt in both Great Britain and its colonies, its subsequent repercussions in America have been multifaceted. While Edwards was a Congregationalist and Whitefield was an Anglican, revivalism in the nineteenth century found expression among the Presbyterians, Baptists, Methodists, Lutherans, Dutch and German Reformed,

2. Tolson, "New," 38.
3. Murray, *Jonathan Edwards*, 214–15.
4. Noll, *American Evangelicalism*, 9.
5. Ibid., 13.

and some Episcopalians. Today many African American churches, independent congregations, and Pentecostal groups would classify themselves as evangelicals.

Interestingly, evangelicalism has both shaped the culture and been shaped by the culture. Noll says the movement has always been *diverse, flexible, adaptable, and multiform.*[6] After the Great Awakening, American evangelicalism became more populist or individualistic in comparison with European Protestantism, which historically could be buttressed by the powers of the state. By contrast, American evangelicalism is sometimes "ambiguous in its appeals to authority and often relies on charismatic leaders or organizational geniuses who (with populist rhetoric) replace traditional autocracy with their own iron discipline."[7] For example, the rise of fundamentalism in the 1920s was largely a leader-lead movement against elements of modernity perceived to be threatening to the faith (e.g., Darwinism and higher criticism of Scripture). Separated from the Northern mainline denominations from which they seceded, fundamentalists developed their own subcultures of colleges, missionary enterprises, and parachurch organizations. The downside of these separatist tendencies was further isolation from the culture evangelicals wanted to influence. During the 1930s many conservative evangelical groups grew faster than the general population, despite being almost invisible to cultural elites and gatekeepers.[8]

Billy Graham is credited with preaching the gospel to a wide-as-possible audience, and in doing so he also sought to break down walls that separated fundamentalists and modernists. Neo-evangelicalism, as it came to be called in the 1950s and 1960s, attempted to revive the "fundamentals" of conservative evangelicalism, but with "a positive spirituality and an intellectual incisiveness that had become rare among militant fundamentalists."[9] The founding of the magazine *Christianity Today* and a host of Christian publishing houses like Baker, Eerdmans, and Zondervan created outlets for Christians who wanted to encourage the faithful and at the same time engage the larger culture.

Noll claims the diversity that has always existed within North American evangelicalism has become more pronounced in recent decades.[10] This

6. Ibid., 14.
7. Ibid., 15.
8. Ibid., 16–18.
9. Ibid., 19.
10. Ibid., 22.

diversity becomes even more apparent when looking at how the movement has attached itself to politics. Black evangelicals have tended to vote Democrat, and conservative White evangelicals have tended to vote Republican. While the elimination of prayer in the public schools in the 1960s and the subsequent legalizing of abortion in 1973 galvanized many conservative evangelicals to be more pro-active in their voting behavior, theological affiliation is not a hard determinate of political affiliation. President Reagan, who was ushered into White House with the help of the religious right, belonged to a liberal church body (Presbyterian Church USA). Jimmy Carter and Bill Clinton, moderately liberal Democrats, both belong to a conservative church body—the Southern Baptist Convention.

Noll reports that with the decline of older, mainline Protestant churches, evangelicals worry less about theological liberalism and more about multiculturalism, postmodernism, and the general secularization of public life.[11] Evangelicals do not always agree on how to best reach an increasingly relativistic culture that shops around for religion in the same way that it surfs for television programs. Because much of modern evangelicalism mirrors, often unconsciously, the same entrepreneurial, individualistic, and pragmatic values that shaped America, corporate-like mega-churches increasingly became the model for successful ministry. David F. Wells of Gordon-Conwell Theological Seminary observes that these new churches sprang up like mushrooms across the American landscape:

> Gone, very often are the familiar church buildings, and in their place are those that look more like low-slung corporate headquarters or country clubs. Inside, a cyclone of change has ripped out the crosses, the pews, the eighteenth-century hymns, the organs, the biblical discourses. In their place are contemporary songs, drums, cinema-grade seats, light discourses, professional singers, drama, and humor.[12]

Not all evangelicals are oblivious to how modernity is reshaping Old World Protestant sensibilities. There exists a small but growing faction within the evangelical community that is deeply concerned about what they see as a capitulation of biblical truth to the priorities of mass culture. Among the disenchanted can be found Baptist, Lutheran, Reformed, Presbyterian, Episcopalian, and independent churches. These evangelical malcontents tend to be both Reformed and confessional in outlook. By Reformed I mean

11. Ibid., 24.

12. Wells, Introduction to *Compromised Church*, 20.

adhering to a certain set of theological distinctives, specifically, the five points of Calvinism and the five "solas" of the Reformation.[13] By confessional I mean adhering to confessional creeds as authoritative declarations of church belief and practice (e.g., the Westminster Confession of Faith).

Henceforth, I refer to these evangelicals as the *Confessionalists*. Like Postman, they are cultural conservatives who have come to realize that older social traditions should not be sacrificed on the altar of *progress*. They are more backward looking than forward, desiring to preserve what they see as the *permanent things* in the culture. Confessionalists are troubled with capitalism's excesses, especially the Church's harnessing of market techniques to procure converts. In this sense, they belong to neither the Protestant left, which devalues doctrinal certainty, nor to the Protestant right, which today is tempted to trivialize doctrinal certainty under a banner of relevance. Founded in 1994, The Alliance of Confessing Evangelicals has been at the forefront of criticizing the hyper-consumerism now prevalent within the evangelical community. The following statement is taken from the Alliance's declaration of purpose:

> In practice, the church is guided, far too often, by the culture. Therapeutic technique, marketing strategies, and the beat of the entertainment world often have far more to say about what the church wants, how it functions and what it offers, than does the Word of God . . . Rather than adapting Christian faith to satisfy the felt needs of consumers, we must proclaim the law as the only measure of true righteousness and the gospel as the only announcement of saving truth.[14]

And this is where Postman enters the evangelical conversation. It is these Reformed, confessional, culture-conscious, and market-leery evangelicals who like to quote Postman. They do so for the simple reason that they agree with much of his assessment of American culture. Postman provides fodder for their critique for what they see as a ravishing of evangelical Christianity. They would give a hardy "Amen" to Postman's claim

---

13. The five points of Calvinism include the theological distinctions of total depravity, unconditional election, definite atonement, irresistible grace, and perseverance of the saints. The five solas of the Reformation include sola scriptura (Scripture alone), sola fide (faith alone), sola gratia (grace alone), solus Christus (Christ alone), and soli deo gloria (for the glory of God alone).

14. Alliance of Confessing Evangelicals, "Cambridge Declaration."

that Christianity is a demanding and serious religion and that "when it is delivered as easy and amusing, it is another religion altogether."[15]

Jewish Enlightenment Media Critic and the Confessionalists

Of course Postman was not an evangelical, but a Jewish humanist. Gregory Reynolds ascribed to him the title, "Jewish Enlightenment Media Critic."[16] The title is helpful, not only because it summarizes Postman's philosophical dispositions, but also because it serves as a basis to compare and contrast his ideas with the Confessionalists.

Postman's analysis of culture was informed by a Jewish sensibility, the natural precursor of a Christian sensibility, especially in light of those theologies that view Christianity as a natural extension of Judaism. Many Christian traditions hold that the New Testament is a form of Jewish Midrashing of the Scriptures—that the New is a fulfillment of the Old. Postman's ideas are attractive to the Confessinalists because of his insistence that both the Jewish and Christian faiths are necessarily logocentric. Even before coming upon McLuhan's now famous axiom, "the medium is the message," Postman said his study of the Bible as a young man helped him to see how "forms of media favor particular kinds of content and therefore are capable of taking command of a culture."[17] He saw how Moses' prohibition against graven images in the Old Testament as entirely intentional, designed to declare a God who was to exist in the Word and through the Word, "an unprecedented conception requiring the highest order of abstract thinking."[18] In a lively conversation with Camille Paglia, captured by *Harper's Magazine*, Postman explained why writing is necessary to conceptualize the nonvisible, nonmaterial God of the Old Testament:

> Writing is the perfect medium because, unlike pictures or the oral tradition, the written word is a symbol system of a symbol system, twice removed from reality and perfect for describing a God who is also far removed from reality: a nonphysical, abstract divinity. Moses smartly chose the right communication strategy. With the Second Commandment [*Thou shalt not make unto thee any graven*

15. Postman, *Amusing Ourselves to Death*, 121.

16. Reynolds, *Word Is Worth a Thousand Pictures*, 171.

17. Postman, *Amusing Ourselves to Death*, 8–9.

18. Ibid., 9.

image], Moses was the first person who ever said, more or less, "Don't watch TV; go do your homework."[19]

This quote reveals Postman's bias toward literacy and cultures that arise out of literacy as well as his respect for Judaism as a viable religious narrative among the other major religions of the world.[20] But Postman was also a defender of the Western Enlightenment philosophical tradition, an outlook that both resonates and at the same time clashes with the absolutism of most Confessionalists. Postman certainly cannot be classified as a biblical literalist, even when he discuses the Old Testament. Postman says *Moses* smartly chose the right medium. He ignores the notion that *God* might have chosen the right medium. (A more literal reading of the Scriptures would place Moses as the recipient of the law, rather than the originator, as stated in Exodus 31:18.) In this sense, Postman saw the Decalogue as a product of human culture rather than a product of Divine Revelation. This is Enlightenment thinking to which Postman was committed and which he articulates in his last book *Building a Bridge to the Eighteenth Century*. Postman is best seen as a traditional humanist in the same strain of public philosophy as Allan Bloom, supporting the Western canon and casting a skeptical eye toward postmodern relativism.

Although traditional humanism would value the importance of major cultural institutions (home, government, and church), Confessionalists would see these institutions as divinely established. Nevertheless, Postman's traditional humanism is more culturally conserving than progressive humanism, which tends to emphasize change. As Reynolds pointed out, Postman was a Post-Kantian thinker who believed in the importance of having a coherent narrative to live one's life.[21] Whether the narrative is *right* or *wrong* in an absolute sense was not his concern. Any narrative was sufficient, so long as it led to a civil and sensible life. Marxism, Darwinism, Fascism, Inductive Science, and Technology with a capital T were exceptions, however, having proved themselves deficient in the last century.[22] In *The End of Education* Postman offers five plausible narratives that students might hang their hats on—The Spaceship Earth (we have an obligation to be good stewards of the planet), The Fallen Angel (we should be creative skeptics toward dogmatism because of the errors humans have made in the

19. Postman and Paglia, "She Wants Her TV," 45.

20. See Gencarelli, "Intellectual Roots," 96.

21. See Reynolds, *Word Is Worth a Thousand Pictures*, 172.

22. See Postman, "Science," 29–32.

past), The American Experiment (the nation's experiment in democracy is a perpetual and fascinating hypothesis in which students must be prepared to participate), The Law of Diversity (human activity is by its very nature diverse and provides a rich set of standards civilized people can adhere), and The Word Weavers / The World Makers (language and the tools of language serve to create our worlds for good or ill). For Postman all these narratives are useful because they each inform the student what it is to be human, to be a responsible citizen, and what it means to be intelligent.[23] One must remember these narratives come as close to a sense of transcendence as Postman could imagine within the context of public schooling.[24]

Confessionalists would see this smorgasbord approach of narrative choosing as somewhat relativistic. But as a proponent of the Enlightenment, Postman valued keeping the question mark in all things rather than answering every query with absolute certainty. Most of the time, that is. He was not afraid to take the high moral ground at the 2000 Media Ecology Association Convention as its keynote speaker, ending his speech with this quip:

> Let me conclude, then, by saying that as I understand the whole point of media ecology, it exists to further our insights into how we stand as human beings, *how we are doing morally* in the journey we are taking. There may be some of you who think of yourselves as media ecologists who disagree with what I have just said. If that is the case, you are *wrong*.[25]

To use such language one has to believe in the terms *better* and *worse*, which the founder of the first graduate program in Media Ecology certainly did. Postman's morality consisted in his beliefs in Jeffersonian democracy, self-evident truths, personal responsibility, free inquiry, clarity of thought, and the notion of civility—components of American-brand traditional humanism. Confessionalists would sympathize with these ideals since many of them believe American democracy grew out of the Reformation as much as it did the Enlightenment. Confessionalists realize that after the founding of the nation, Reformation and Enlightenment values split, one going the way of revivalism and the other going the way of naturalistic materialism as embodied in Postman's science god. If Postman would have us return to the ethos of the eighteenth century, most Confessionalists would not (I

---

23. Postman, *End of Education*, 60.
24. Ibid., 62.
25. Postman, "Humanism."

believe) think this an entirely bad idea. After all, it was an era in which both Benjamin Franklin *and* Jonathan Edwards thrived.

Postman did not wear his religion on his shirtsleeves, but he was keenly aware of the role religion played in shaping culture and its importance in giving meaning to our existence. He was a public philosopher who believed in public education and the permissibility of comparative religion in the classroom.[26] He also acknowledged the influence of religion on other media ecologists like Marshall McLuhan, Jacques Ellul, and Walter Ong. Postman once told Reynolds in a personal interview, "I am uncertain as to whether God has spoken, but I am going to live life as if God spoke, in part because if I don't believe this, I will lose my way."[27] He seems to laud traditional family values in *Building a Bridge to the Eighteenth Century* when he speaks of the "depressing" fact the "structure and authority of the family have been severely weakened as parents have lost control over the information environment of the young."[28] And when he declares, "If parents wish to preserve childhood for their own children, they must conceive of parenting as an act of rebellion against culture,"[29] he sounds like a right-wing Christian evangelical if ever there was one.

Postman was a critic of contemporary American culture in Socratic fashion, an occupation that finds common ground with the intellectual ebullience of the Reformed tradition—a pursuit that encourages a certain dialectic of affirmation and negation towards culture, society, and the self. Of course, anyone who persistently questions what hardly anyone else questions at all, is a Socratic. In this sense, all the Reformers were Socratics because they questioned culturally-imbedded norms that few others questioned. Luther and Calvin and Zwingli were trying to pull their worlds back to a biblical equilibrium, thermostatically. Likewise, when Postman barks that television is the first curriculum in the life of a child, he is in effect nailing his Theses on the door of the Castle Church at Technopolis. He is making us think about things we had not consciously thought about before: what we perceived to be normal in our environment. Postman is saying television is common, but it is not normal.

26. Postman, *Building a Bridge to the Eighteenth Century*, 171–73.
27. Reynolds, *Word Is Worth a Thousand Pictures*, 172.
28. Postman, *Building a Bridge to the Eighteenth Century*, 128.
29. Ibid., 129.

Some Confessional Evangelicals Who Quote Postman

The following is a sample of evangelical scholarship that relies heavily on Postman's work. The list, in alphabetical order, is representative rather than exhaustive. I have included the church affiliation of each writer along with his or her particular vocation. Each scholar fits the description of a Confessionalist—Reformed, creedal in faith profession, culture-conscious, and market-leery in regard to church practice.

Marva J. Dawn, Theologian, Musician, Educator (Lutheran)

Dawn is Teaching Fellow in Spiritual Theology at Regent College in Vancouver, British Columbia. Her book, *Reaching Out without Dumbing Down: A Theology of Worship for Turn-of-the-Century Culture*, is a "why to" manual for Protestant liturgy amidst the heat surrounding the worship wars. Dawn did her dissertation at Notre Dame on the ideas of Jacques Ellul. She quotes Postman extensively, recognizing with him that religion has been recast in television's terms. Rewriting Postman's foreword in *Amusing Ourselves to Death*, Dawn says, "When the congregation becomes an audience and its worship a vaudeville act, then the Church finds itself at risk; the death of faith and Christian character is a clear possibility."[30] She mourns television's assault on exposition in which the Church historically has been dependent for teaching doctrines and creeds. Dawn believes "television has habituated its watchers to a low information-action ratio, that people are accustomed to 'learning' good ideas (even from sermons) and then doing nothing about them."[31] Noting Postman's observation that television decontextualizes information, she asserts current trends in worship decontextualizes or muddles Christian doctrine. Function not only follows form in television, but also in worship as style is valued over substance and symbol drain in the culture at large makes religious symbols lose their significance. She would have Protestants think deeply about their liturgies and avoid making worship a matter of entertaining an audience. However, these warnings do not preclude worship that contains imagination, a sense of drama, and spiritual vitality.

---

30. Dawn, *Reaching Out Without Dumbing Down*, 13.
31. Ibid., 21.

Os Guinness, Writer and Speaker
(Episcopalian in the Reformed Tradition)

Guinness is cofounder of the Trinity Forum, a seminar-style forum for senior executives and political leaders that engages the leading ideas of our
day in the context of faith. Although the author of numerous books on
topics ranging from vocation to what he sees as the over-valued status of
relevance in contemporary culture, his most Postman-embracing work is
*Fit Bodies, Fat Minds: Why Evangelicals Don't Think And What To Do About
It*. Guinness is appalled at the anti-intellectualism within American evangelicalism which manifests itself in such areas as a low regard to authority,
tradition, liturgical worship, aesthetics, and a constructive public policy.
A major chunk of the book falls under a section titled "An Idiot Culture"
and includes these media-ecology-friendly chapters: "Amusing Ourselves
to Death," "All Consuming Images," "The Humiliation of the Word," and
"Real, Reel, or Virtually Real?" Guinness claims Postman's *Amusing Ourselves to Death* is probably "the best single introduction to the issue" of the
influence of television on reading and thinking.[32] He touches upon many
of Postman's claims about television—that we have shifted from the age of
exposition to the age of entertainment, that all subject matter on television
is presented as entertainment, that television discourse has a bias against
understanding because it is fast-paced and fragmented, that it has a bias
against responsibility because it prevents the viewer from engaging with
the consequences of what is experienced, that it has a bias against memory
and history because of its preoccupation with the here and now, and that it
has a bias against truth and accuracy because it turns credibility into plausibility and performance. Guinness holds that these biases have dramatically
affected Protestant evangelicalism:

> So evangelicals have followed suit [accepting visual culture un
> questioningly] and abandoned their Reformed heritage. At the
> highest levels this shift has opened the door to the more pictorial
> theology of Eastern Orthodoxy. At the lower levels it has wel
> comed in trash and what is worse—idolatry.[33]

32. Guinness, *Fit Bodies, Fat Minds*, 76.
33. Ibid., 99.

Kenneth Myers, Radio Host
(Episcopalian in the Reformed Tradition)

Myers is host and producer of the Mars Hill Audio Journal, a bimonthly audio magazine that examines issues in contemporary culture form a framework shaped by Christian conviction. In Myers book, *All God's Children and Blue Suede Shoes: Christians & Popular Culture*, he explores the origins, functions, and influences of popular culture on Americans in general and Christians in particular. He relies most heavily on Postman in a chapter entitled "Popular Culture's Medium: The Entertainment Appliance." Myers says television is an "assumed medium" that no one complains about any longer.[34] As proof, he says no leading educator seems willing to endorse the arguments of Postman or that of Jerry Mander (*Four Arguments for the Elimination of Television*) or Marie Winn (*The Plug-In Drug*).[35] "Television is . . . not simply the dominant medium of popular culture," says Myers. "It is the single most significant shared reality in our entire society."[36] Myers shares Postman's assessment of television when he says images are insufficient to communicate abstraction and analysis and therefore fight against the distinction between truth and falsehood.[37] Television discourages reflection, erodes our sense of important social spaces, and distorts our sense of time.[38] The problem would not be as complicated for the Church as it is, but evangelicals have embraced many of the forms of popular culture to promote its message.[39] Myers suggests that Christians can enjoy popular culture so long as they are not "dominated by the sensibility of popular culture" which is the same as being "captivated by its idols."[40] Parents, teachers, and church leaders can do much for those under their care in establishing a cultural sensibility that is more reflective and discerning.

34. Myers, *All God's Children*, 159.
35. Ibid.
36. Ibid., 160.
37. Ibid., 162–64.
38. Ibid., 170–72.
39. Ibid., 181.
40. Ibid., 180.

Gene Edward Veith, Provost, Patrick Henry College (Lutheran)

Veith, Provost of Patrick Henry College and Director of the Cranch Institute at Concordia Theological Seminary, quotes Postman extensively in his books addressing the problems associated with postmodernism. In *Reading Between the Lines: Christian Guide to Literature*, Veith refers to Postman as one of the "most astute social critics of our time."[41] The first chapter of the book, "The Word and the Image: The Importance of Reading," introduces a basic media ecology presupposition—that different forms of communication shape people's thinking and ultimately the culture. As with the Jewish faith, reading is essential to Christianity because it is a religion centered around a Book (the Greek word for *Bible* is "the Book"). Veith says Christians derive their conversation with God from this Book: "In the Bible, God reveals His relationship to us, setting forth the law by which we should live and the gospel of forgiveness through Christ. As we read the Bible, God addresses us in the most intimate way, as one person speaking to another."[42] Veith reiterates one of Postman's most acute questions about image culture: "Can democratic institutions survive without literacy if they arose out of literacy?" Veith summarizes Postman's concern that an image culture bears the consequences of losing a sense of authority and history, can be hostile to rationality, and is prone to pleasure-centeredness.

Some of these same themes are echoed in another book by Veith, *Postmodern Times: A Christian Guide to Contemporary Thought and Culture*,[43] a work that received a *Christianity Today* book award. Veith traces the intellectual, historical, and technological roots of postmodernism, contrasting it with modernity. Veith says that although electronic media are the product of modernist rationalism, it ironically assaults the rationalism of modernism. Relying heavily on Postman's *Technopoly: The Surrender of Culture to Technology*, Veith notes that emerging information technologies, and those who control them, form a new socio-political order. In this sense, Veith agrees with Postman that technology is often at odds with tradition. Specifically, electronic media erodes high culture and makes the profane common place.

One of the more interesting pieces of scholarship produced by Veith is *Modern Fascism: Liquidating the Judeo-Christian Worldview*. The primary

41. Veith, *Reading Between the Lines*, 20.

42. Ibid., 18.

43. Veith, *Postmodern Times*.

thesis of the book suggests that the replacement of rational debate with media manipulation, the subordination of logic to emotionalism, and the trivalization of politics, all tenets of our popular culture, form a fertile breeding ground for new forms of fascism. Veith points out that fascism has stood in opposition to the Judeo-Christian worldview because of its rejection of a transcendent God and His moral law. For example, Nazism under Hitler sought to recapture the mythological consciousness of the old pagan order via divine king, sacred community, communion with nature, and the sacrifice of blood. Veith's concern is that when transcendent values are excluded from a culture, politics can become reduced to sheer "will to power." And if there are no absolutes, no basis for moral persuasion or rational argument, then power becomes arbitrary, allowing the side with the biggest propaganda machine and the dirtiest tactics to win. In *Modern Facism* Veith relies on Postman to show how electronic media, particularly television, has eroded linear logic, sustained inquiry, tradition, and deferred gratification.[44]

Conclusion

Confessionalists see the burgeoning image culture as a threat to their word-based heritage. Not all evangelicals recognize the societal repercussions of electronic media because many of them operate under a paradigm of pragmatism. Evangelicals attach their efforts to build the Kingdom with the same market values that dominate consumer culture, hoping to be as successful. Those evangelicals who *do* recognize the dangers see themselves as taking up the mantles of Luther and Calvin in decrying idolatry—worshipping the creature over the Creator. Postman is entirely handy for the Confessionalist because he knew a golden calf when he saw one.

44. Veith, *Modern Fascism*, 145–46.

3

The Image Versus the Word—
Old Story, New Twist

A Lament from a Christian Media Ecologist

Little children, keep yourselves from idols.[1]

HERE ARE THREE DEFINITIONS of idolatry, one from a poet, one from an apostle, and one from a college professor. The first is plucked from William Blake's *Marriage of Heaven and Hell*:

The ancient Poets animated all sensible objects with Gods . . .

Till a system was formed . . .

And at length they pronounced that the Gods had order'd such things.

Thus men forgot that All deities reside in the human breast.

According to Blake all gods sprang from the human brow. Unfortunately, Blake believed this about the Judeo-Christian God as well. I will forgive him on that point for the moment so I can apply his observation to the chief competitor of the Judeo-Christian God, paganism. Blake is saying that once the poets of old had animated the objects of nature in literature and in art, had used pen and chisel to transform animals and people into deities, a religious system conveniently ensued.

The second definition of idolatry comes to us from the Apostle Paul and is not too far removed from Blake's estimation: "Professing themselves to be wise, they became fools, and changed the glory of the incorruptible God into an image made like to corruptible man—and birds and

---

1. 1 John 5:21 NKJV.

four-footed animals and creeping things . . . and worshiped and served the creature rather than the Creator . . ."[2] The Greeks took what knowledge they had of God, however limited, and failed to honor Him in the way He had been revealed. In turn, they devised gods to meet their own appetites. In other words, Paul is saying that idolatry is the *suppression* and the *recasting* of God. The pagans were not seeking God, but running away from Him. They were worshipping the god of their own minds.

The last definition of idolatry is from Camille Paglia and it parallels my own understanding of the biblical concept of *Babylon*. In her book, *Sexual Personae*, Paglia says that idolatry is best understood as "fascism of the eye"—"pictorialism plus the will-to-power. It is ritualism, gradiosity, colossalism, sensationalism."[3]

According to this definition, pagan idolatry is more than falling down in front of a totem pole. It is Nimrod spouting off atop the world's first skyscraper. It is the pharaoh-headed lion transfixed in desert sand and Nebuchadnezzar's ninety-foot effigy of himself. It is Alexander elbowing his way onto Mount Olympus and Nero lighting his garden with human torches. It is power and style and person worship expressed visibly, and ultimately politically, through the *image*.

Paglia says paganism has made a very nice comeback. Note her characteristic audacity in *Personae*:

> The twentieth century is not the Age of Anxiety but the Age of Hollywood. The pagan cult of personality has reawakened and dominates all art, all thought. It is morally empty but ritually profound. . . . Movie screen and television are its sacred precincts.[4]

And:

> With the rebirth of the gods in the massive idolatries of popular culture, with the eruption of sex and violence into every corner of the ubiquitous mass media, Judeo-Christianity is facing its most serious challenge since Europe's confrontation with Islam in the Middle Ages. The latent paganism of western culture has burst forth again in all daemonic vitality.[5]

---

2. Rom 1: 22–23, 25 NKJV.

3. Paglia, *Sexual Personae*, 139.

4. Ibid., 32.

5. Ibid., 25.

Now to talk like this you have to believe that Christianity is in some kind of trouble. This essay attempts to address the nature of the trouble Paglia speaks of but from the perspective of someone who mourns the trouble. While Paglia believes Christianity is facing its most serious challenge in a thousand years, she is not really crying about it. I am crying about it. When she uses terms like *pagan cult of personality* and *massive idolatries* she is referring to the values of decadent Rome—sex, violence, and celebrity—which she believes is the *natural* way of the world. And she is right of course if we are talking about Babylon.

Words and Theological Complexity

But Christianity has never has claimed to be a *natural* way. The saints of the Bible were a particular people because they were an interrupted people. Abraham, Moses, and Paul were interrupted to speak for God—to get His message out. To further extend this point, if one holds to a more literal interpretation of the Bible then it stands to reason that God interrupted the saints to make them sit down and write down that message. Which is to say, when God took the initiative to reach down to mankind, it was no mistake that he purposefully chose the medium of writing to make himself known.

There are two basic reasons for this. First, writing is the ideal medium to describe an abstract divinity.[6] Blocks of stone and paint are just insufficient to convey things like holiness, mercy, self-existence, eternality, sovereignty, omniscience, omnipotence, and omnipresence. Writing has *objectivity* and *permanency*. Objectivity is essential because both writing and God are removed from reality—they both transcend. Writing is actually twice removed from reality because it is a symbol system (letters) of a symbol system (speech). Writing enables the reader to *see* an unseen Being who speaks to us in *words*. Permanency is essential because the Bible is essentially a document of God at work among His people over an extended period of time. Writing allows us to examine the past and compare it with the present in order to have some discernment in preparing for the future.

The second reason God chose the medium of writing is connected with the first and is at the crux of his prohibition against idolatry. Simply stated, writing prevents people from worshipping God as a visible deity. Idolatry is forbidden in the Scriptures because God is above nature and not a part of it. Therefore, in the Decalogue the first commandment requires of

6. See Postman and Paglia, "She Wants Her TV," 45.

us a singular devotion instead of multiple ones, and the second command-ment forbids image worship.

Out of absolute theological necessity, Judaism and Christianity are word-dependent in contrast to paganism, which is image-dependent. Pagan idolatry is Biblicism's chief competitor because one thrives in the absence of the written word and the other cannot exist without it. The Hebrews were the *only* people in antiquity to attempt to teach *everyone* how to read. Although the Hebrews have a strong oral tradition, literacy underpinned memory because these people were charged with being the stewards of Scripture. Not only were the priests and scribes capable of read-ing and writing, but epigraphic discoveries—texts, public inscriptions on buildings, letter seals, personal notes on potsherds—show that the average Israelite was functionally literate as early as the period of the judges.[7]

Idolatry's Convenient Medium

In contrast to Israel's functional literacy, in pagan cultures writing was used to make the bureaucratic engines run smoother and was restricted to a privileged class. Writing was stuck near the top of the pyramid so that the common Egyptian lived and moved among images. For example, Ramses II scattered his personal likeness all over Egypt so no one would doubt he was the big dog of the desert. And in Greece it would be difficult to say that the Athenians achieved general literacy because 80 percent of the population did not actively participate in the polis. What we *can* say of the Greeks is that they gave us our alphabet, the study of rhetoric and philosophy, and our modern concept of the school, all of which aided their experiments with democracy.

But the Greeks also gave us the scandalous god-athletes of Mount Olympus where one saw them in sundry shapes committing heady riots, incest, and rapes.[8] The Greeks also gave the world Alexander, who required those he conquered to call him Mr. God. So while it is true that the Greeks had analytical components in their culture, they also had Dionysian ele-ments as well.

For Rome, the Dionysian dynamic prevailed as well, especially to-ward the end of the empire when the Republic was replaced with emperor

7. See Millard, "Practice of Writing," 98–111. See also Millard, "Question of Israelite Literacy," 29.

8. Boardman et al., *Oxford History of the Classical World*, 261.

worship. Imperial Rome came to permit more than the Greeks would have ever allowed. The Coliseum, the animals, the mock battles, the gladiators, the dwarfs, the public sex, the lion-fed Christians, the vomitoria—all these scene props demonstrate that spectacle finally won out in Rome.

Rome fell, but paganism remained intact. The person worship was only repackaged. As Europe slipped into a dismal night, the gods quietly returned and positioned themselves over the church altar. While it is true that Constantine ended the persecution of the saints with his policy of toleration, he also set in motion the conditions by which pagans and other dissenters would later be persecuted by Christians. Wholesale conversions came rather easy under physical threat.[9] Not everyone understood their faith, and hearts were not necessarily changed. By the fifth century there existed a great diversity of unlearned people, loosely assembled under the banner of Christianity. A good number of them saw no reason to dispense with their old gods. Bishops were willing to make some serious compromises. Pagan festivities were rechristened under a new calendar. Churches were built directly on the foundations of pagan temples where only a short time before prayers to Zeus had been offered. The statues over the church altars were supposed to be that of Jesus and Mary, but they somehow closely resembled Horus, the Egyptian sky god and Isis, the god of royalty.[10] The old paganism and Christianity were visually reconciled. Even the Christian emperors were iconified and deified. The entire progression, writes William Manchester in *A World Lit Only by Fire*, went something like this: "Imperial Rome having yielded to barbarians, and then barbarism to Christianity, Christianity was in turn infiltrated, and to a considerable extent subverted, by the paganism it was supposed to destroy."[11]

During all of this, the analytical elements once embedded in the Roman culture faded off the scene. Literacy faded. Education faded. Civility faded. Sometime after AD 400 darkness swallowed up the Empire. For five hundred years, the ability to read and write was practically unknown.[12] Literacy remained at top of the organizational chart where the clergy comprised an elite social class. Ignorance enabled the Catholic Church to keep control over a large and diverse population.[13] Religion was reduced to image worship and

9. For a full account of "evangelistic inducements" during the waning years of the Roman Empire see MacMullen, *Christianity & Paganism*.

10. Manchester, *World Lit Only by Fire*, 13.

11. Ibid., 11.

12. See Postman, *Disappearance of Childhood*, 14.

13. Ibid., 12.

superstition. Once again, political power was centralized in Rome where, to use the Augustinian phrase, gold, force, and Venus ruled.

New Testament Christianity faded, in part because the *word* faded. If the spirit of the Apostles were to revive again it would have to revive under a return to the Book. And that is precisely what happened. Gutenberg's printing press harnessed Biblicism to a new communication technology to place the Scriptures directly into the hands of the common man. Seven years before Luther nailed his Ninety-five Theses to the door of Church at Wittenberg the tonsured monk visited Rome. The closer he got to the Holy City, the more unholy things appeared. At the papal court he was served supper by twelve naked girls. It makes one pause and think. "If there is a hell," Luther later said, "Rome is built over it."[14]

The Renaissance sought to revive pagan Rome and therefore naturally careened toward the *image*. It was not just the words of the Greek philosophers that inspired them. Villas were built again in the classical mode. Artists brought to life on canvas and in sculpture the myths of ancient antiquity. Whereas the Middle Age made an attempt to disguise the old gods in Christian garb, the Renaissance stripped off their clothes, figuratively and literally, to expose them again in living color. As the Reformation heated up in the north, the High Renaissance was absorbed in spectacle.

A Revival of the Word

Elizabeth Eisenstein notes in *The Printing Revolution in Early Modern Europe* that "Luther had invited a public disputation and nobody had come to dispute. Then by a stroke of magic he found himself addressing the whole world."[15] Erasmus observed that Luther's books were everywhere and in every language. By 1534, Luther had produced a German Bible. What Luther did for Germany William Tyndale did for England by translating the New Testament into the vernacular for which he was burned at the stake. Tyndale's last words were said to have been: "Lord, open the king of England's eyes." Three years later English Bibles sat in every parish church in the country. Daniel Defoe, the author who gave us the narrative of a man alone with the Bible, would later declare: "The preaching of sermons is speaking to a few of mankind [but] printing books is talking to the whole world."[16]

14. Durant, *Reformation*, 344.

15. Eisenstein, *Printing Revolution*, 153.

16. Ibid., 157.

Calvin, Knox, Locke, and others raised notions about inalienable rights, government by consent, and separation of powers. Europe was set on fire. The printing press was the mechanical engine that drove the Reformation. In turn, the Reformation was a part of the impetus for the spread of literacy, education, modern science, and democracy.

America was born out of a print-oriented culture. Early Americans possessed what Neil Postman refers to as a "typographical mind," that is, a mind shaped by the habit of reading. Having submitted to the "sovereignty of the printing press," says Postman, the typographical mind had "a sophisticated ability to think conceptually, deductively and sequentially; a high valuation of reason and order; and abhorrence of contradiction; a large capacity for detachment and objectivity; and a tolerance for delayed response."[17] The fruit of all this was an information environment in which people paid attention—*could* pay attention—could pay attention to public debates, could discern between logical and emotional appeals, could pay attention to *words*. The Founding Fathers did their work in an information environment forged by the printing press and spirited by the fires of the Reformation. Despite their wisdom, however, the Fathers did not foresee an age in which moving pictures would come to subvert the written word.

The Graphic Revolution:
Photography, Cinema, Radio, and Television

Philosopher Bertrand Russell once observed how the effect of the Industrial Revolution had been one of making instruments to make other instruments, to make still other instruments. In regards to the entertainment industry, this was especially true. The photograph, the moving picture, the radio, and the television set were built on top of each other, technically speaking. Ironically, they all ended up in the hands of showmen. Each machine became plugged into the visceral rawness of life that the new tenets of modernism seemed to call forth.

Writing in *The Atlantic Monthly* in 1859, Oliver Wendell Holmes keenly observed that the photograph marked the beginning of an era where the image would become more important than the object itself: "Every conceivable object of Nature and Art will soon scale off its surface for us. Men will hunt all curious, beautiful, grand objects, as they hunt cattle in South

---

17. Postman, *Amusing Ourselves to Death*.

America, for their skins and leave the carcasses as little worth."[18] In newspapers and magazines, the picture screamed for the attention and prompted exposition to take second seat. The photograph *became* our exposition in advertising, publicity, and propaganda and helped create the pseudo-event (an event designed only to call attention to itself.)[19]

In 1907, there were 2,500 movie theaters in America. Seven years later there were seven million.[20] What young urbanites found on the big screen were attractive role-models to help them cope with all manner of "anxieties" they faced while living in a lonely crowd. D. W. Griffith, the man who first understood the power of the close-up, broke the distance between audience and actor so that the viewer could look upon every facial feature, every line, every subtle expression of the eyes and mouth. Hollywood cranked out celebrities like Ford cranked out cars. Actors were put under contract, fashioned by the studio, and paraded across the screen: Gary Cooper, Bette Davis, James Cagney, Spencer Tracy, Katharine Hepburn, Fred Astaire, Ginger Rogers, Humphrey Bogart, Judy Garland and on and on. No longer would the average American look out and see an empty wilderness to shape by his own design, says Christopher Lasch in *The Culture of Narcissism*; our membership in the cult of celebrity made us look out and see the world as a mirror. Loneliness and anxiety were conquered by gazing upon a "grandiose self" as reflected in those who radiated "celebrity, power, and charisma."[21]

In his *Poetics* Aristotle wrote that spectacle was a type of attraction in itself, but it is the least artistic and the least connected with the art of poetry (by "poetry" he was referring to Greek tragedy as performed on the stage). To put it another way, theater can occur without elaborate scenery. But the opposite view prevailed in film. Homer took to the silver screen in a big way. Cinema is one of our favorite rituals and probably ranks in value somewhere up there with church attendance. In essence, cinema is theater—BIG THEATER. The movie camera amplifies stage action and allows for dazzling action—a ripping tornado, a fire-breathing dinosaur, a landing spacecraft, an exploding White House. Raw vividness is the dominant value in film today so that the monsters must be even more hideous than the last

18. Holmes, "Stereoscope," 25.

19. Boorstin coined the term "pseudo-event" in *The Image*.

20. Czitrom, *Media and the American Mind*, 41–42.

21. Lasch, *Culture of Narcissism*, 38.

one, the blood must spurt farther, the explosion must be more brilliant, and the body count must be higher.

Radio also relied on excitable personalities, even if we could not see them. The product of telephone and wireless technologies, radio began as vaudeville in a box and served to get the Depression off people's minds. Taken together with the movies, Americans now lost themselves in a fantasy world on a regular basis. For the first time in the nation's history, people began to see entertainment as a major part of their lives. The introduction of television tribalized radio, making it a bonding agent for the youth culture and pouring forth a long line of rock-and-roll personalities—Elvis, Jerry Lee Lewis, the Beatles. The music industry remains celebrity and image-driven and has largely been given over to a content of sex and in-your-face tantalization.

"We shall stand or fall by television—of that I am quite sure," remarked E. B. White in 1938.[22] A year later President Roosevelt's image was dispersed from aerials atop the Empire State Building in the first commercial broadcast that coincided with the World's Fair in New York City. Reflecting on the societal impact of television was the fair's science director, Gerald Wendt, who wrote, "Democracy, under the influence of television, is likely to pay inordinate attention to the performer and interpreter rather than to the planner and thinker."[23]

As Postman has pointed out in his book *Amusing Ourselves to Death*, television's ultimate proposition is whether serious public discourse can be carried out via a medium that is always seeking to entertain. If the printing press could provide a new impetus for public conversations, one that was sane and rational, what on earth would be unleashed on us if we shifted all this over to moving pictures? What would happen if politics, education, and religion became a kind of song and dance routine? Could a pro wrestler be elected to a high political office? Would students demand that their teachers be entertaining above everything else? Would churches stop preaching and start entertaining? And the scary thing is that we have only begun our dance with images. The great eye machines were booted up only a century ago.

22. Goldstein, *History of Television*, 15.
23. Gelernter, *1939*, 167.

Pagan Piety

We are not too different from the Egyptians or the Greeks or the Romans or the suffering masses living in the Dark Ages that idolized their gods. Today the average American adult sees approximately five hundred advertisements each day and by the time a person reaches twenty-one years of age, he or she will be exposed to between one and two million ad messages.[24] We live now in a house of mirrors so that one cannot turn around without seeing his or hers most base desires in iconic form. The pagans saw themselves in myth and marble: what they wanted to be, what they strove for—a diverse assortment of human activity and passion on a grandiose scale. Art was just the vehicle whereby they worshipped *themselves*. The German philosopher Friedrich Nietzsche, a student of the Greek imagination and a favorite philosopher of Hitler, wrote in *The Birth of Tragedy* that once the gods had been cast in their various roles and placed upon the stage of Mount Olympus, the Greeks began to emulate them. Pagan piety was never that of Judaism or Christianity. The relationship between man and his gods was a casual one—festivity not sanctimony. The gods delighted in seeing humans enjoy themselves. Therefore, singing, dancing, athletics, crudity, obscenity, and the occasional orgy accompanied the blood sacrifice.

Again, Blake's point is pertinent here: Once the creature has been animated, a larger culture will follow. The *Image* seeks not only religious devotion but also a political life. We have seen it before, in Egypt, in Greece, in Rome, in the Dark Ages, and most recently in Germany under Adolf Hitler. One way Hitler can be explained is by the circumstance of the *vanishing word*. Germany's bout with demagoguery is a story of the vanishing word with a capital "W" as well as a lower case "w." The rejection of the Jews, and ultimately the dissenting Christians, was in larger scope, a rejection of a transcendent God and His transcendent laws. Hitler found little merit in *the* Word or in *words* because Hitler himself became the *Word* and *images* under the name of propaganda naturally made him a better object of devotion.

The allure of idolatry is one of oldest stories in the world. Just ponder for a moment the history of Israel in the Old Testament. We are really all pagans at heart. It *is* the natural way. For a while a robust Biblicism kept Babylon outside the door, but the gods are back in town. Although it might be controversial to say it, postmodernism has more in common with fascism than with its totalitarian competitor of communism because

24. Wilson and Wilson, *Mass Media, Mass Culture*, 344.

so much that characterizes our age is a turning *from* rationality, and at the same time, an embracing *of* spectacle. As Gene Veith explains in his book *Modern Fascism*, the replacement of rational debate with media manipulation, the subordination of logic to emotionalism, and the trivialization of politics—all tenets of our popular culture—form a fertile breeding ground for a new kind of fascism.[25] We seem to be safe for now, but the future arrives much faster these days, and the world is rapidly shrinking, and we can now blow each other up quite easily. Such a landscape presents marvelous opportunities for political sophistry.

There exists a long-standing and irreconcilable tension between the *word* and the *image*. The devaluation of the *word* and its hostile supplanting by the *image* poses a direct assault upon "the religion of the Book" as well as what that religion helped to produce—literacy, civility, and in America's case, a consitutional democracy. If the spirit of the Apostles is to revive again, it has to revive under a return to the *Word* in general and *words* in particular. This would mean reconditioning our fingers to turn pages instead of punching the television clicker. It would mean teaching others not only what our new technologies can do *for* us, but also what they are doing *to* us. It might even mean giving the "worship as entertainment" paradigm the big hook. Perhaps Christians would do well to give serious consideration to yanking the multicolored, high-tech give-me show off the church stage and get back to something more Bookish.

25. Veith, *Modern Fascism*, 12–13.

4

Why I Am Not Going to Teach Public Speaking Online

I'm not used to talking to somebody in a body.

—U2, "FAST CARS"

I MUST CONFESS FROM the beginning that the inspiration for this piece is derived from Wendell Berry's essay "Why I am not going to buy a computer."[1]
Unlike Berry, however, I own a computer and even composed these words
using one. My intention is not to eschew all technologies, or urge you to do
so, since that would make me some kind of hypocrite. Neither was it Berry's
intention, for he maintained that his current technologies—a pencil, pad,
and a 1956 Royal standard typewriter—were perfectly suited for his purposes. He said that until somebody demonstrated how a computer could
produce better writing than Dante's he would not buy one. It is in this spirit
that I make my claim.

There are many colleges and universities that are now offering public
speaking online and believe it's an entirely good idea. Several institutions of
higher learning in my state are now doing so, and at my university we allow
such courses to transfer. A colleague, whose office door is less than ten feet
from mine, told me that she was "forced" to teach public speaking online at
a nearby community college. Thankfully, our department has received no
such decree—yet. Not that our department hasn't been asked. Fortunately,
where I teach, faculty still have some ownership of the curriculum, and
thus far we have resisted all inducements.

1. Berry, "Why I Am Not Going to Buy a Computer," 170–77.

Educators are quick to board the online bandwagon. Many schools offer programs where students can earn a complete degree online. At my own university one can earn a Bachelor of Science degree in Agriculture entirely online. It is my understanding that Yale Law School is sharing resources with the "University of the People," a school of higher education that is not only totally online, but tuition-free. Then there is the cop played by Will Farrell in the movie *The Other Guys* who tries to prevent a desperate person from jumping off a window ledge. "I took an online class at the University of Phoenix on negotiating," shouts Farrell. "I'm gonna need a priest and a blow horn."

The guy jumped.

Without a doubt online education is the wave of the future, and I am sure there is some merit in being able to sit at home or the south of France and earn college credit. The justifications are familiar—it is convenient, cheap, and a way to get more students. However, it is naive to think that any course can be taught online. Should sculpting be taught online? Should tennis? Not all subjects translate equally. My reasons for refusing to teach public speaking online are pragmatic, pedagogical, as well as philosophical. Moreover, the trend toward placing great portions of the curriculum online raise a host of questions faculty and administrators should be discussing openly.

If It Ain't Broken

There are three major reasons why I am not going to teach public speaking online. First, the way I currently teach public speaking works extremely well. I have been teaching public speaking at the college level since 1994 and have listened to thousands of speeches presented by young people. Gratefully, my student evaluations have remained high, and I have received a number of awards for my teaching efforts. This is not to say that I have arrived or can learn nothing from new methods. Indeed, I reevaluate my course content and teaching methods constantly, and try to improve each year. But I have come to a place in my profession where I do not feel as though I am groping in the dark.

Please do not mistake these comments as arrogance. My confidence does not reside entirely in my own aptitude, such as it is. But I know there have been many others before me who were entirely successful at transmitting the art of public speaking. You might call me old fashioned in that way; it is a comfort to know that I don't have to reinvent the art. We stand on the shoulders of many other teachers of public speaking—rhetoricians, if you will forgive the older term—that tower down below me for thousands of years.

We could begin with Corax, perhaps the first speech teacher in Western history, who taught the citizens of Sicily how to argue their court cases to reclaim their property from a tyrant. Isocates was another early teacher of oratory. He set up his own school and trained students to write, practice, and deliver speeches. Of course we cannot forget Aristotle, the father of Rhetoric, who said understanding the available means of persuasion involved *ethos* (the credibility of the speaker), *logos* (the use of logical appeals), and *pathos* (connecting with the values of the audience). Moving from the Greek to Roman influence we find Cicero whose political speeches cost him his life. Mark Anthony's wife hated Cicero's tongue so much that she pulled it out of his decapitated head and stabbed it repeatedly. I use Cicero's canons of rhetoric today to teach the speech process to my students: invention, arrangement, style, memory, and delivery. Saint Augustine, a former teacher of Rhetoric, adapted Cicero's ideas in forming his philosophy of Christian education. George Campbell's *Philosophy of Rhetoric* and *Lectures of Pulpit Eloquence* were staples for teachers of oratory around the time America won her independence. The ability to speak effectively was a necessity for anyone going into law, politics, or the ministry. As higher education became more widespread and democratic, universities developed speech departments to accommodate more students. It was generally agreed upon that speech training produced better citizens.

So this has been going on for some time now. Public speaking was successfully taught before the Internet, telegraphy, or the printing press. But *how* was it taught? It was taught the way most all other subjects were taught—orally. Traditional teaching was oral. I am defining orality as it has normally been defined—face-to-face interaction between two or more people. Gilbert Highet says in *The Art of Teaching* that there are three main methods of communicating knowledge from teacher to pupil: lecturing, tutoring, and preliminary student work.[2] All of these methods have an oral aspect if applied to teaching public speaking. I will briefly touch upon each.

There is something I have noticed about Information Technology Service departments. They are constantly encouraging faculty to post their lecture notes online so students can have free access to them. My students are quick to put on their pouty faces when they learn the only place they can find my lecture notes is in the classroom. They also put on their pouty

2. Highet, *Art of Teaching*, 87–88.

faces when I tell them class attendance is mandatory. I suppose the students could photocopy last semester's notes and then just sit there with nothing to write down during class. While some of them might do that, I tell them there is a benefit in carefully listening to a lecture and writing down what they perceive most essential. The discipline fosters critical listening, something we are trying to teach them in public speaking anyway.

I have no empirical evidence to support it, but I suspect many enthusiasts of online education would like to do away with the lecture altogether; they see it is an outmoded form of teaching in the digital age; they think students find lectures boring. Granted, there is nothing worse than a poorly delivered lecture, but this fact only supports keeping the public speaking course robust—so our students will not graduate and then end-up putting to sleep their employees when giving an annual address.

The line of reason offered by many online advocates within higher education goes something like this: The electronic age has created a new kind of student, one who no longer can pay attention to long talks. The solution to this problem is to do away with long talks. Students do not want to listen to boring professors; they want to "be active." What we need to do is give them what they are already familiar with—buttons and pictures. They will enjoy pushing and looking. Education will once again become enjoyable. Software programs can be produced to accommodate them— programs that are intuitive and do not require a lot of reading or listening to boring talks.

If this description is accurate then educators are offering a technical solution for a predicament caused by technology itself, a situation, perhaps, that is analogous to putting a fire out with gasoline. If there is indeed a downside to our digital technology then perhaps we need to be asking ourselves if sustained inquiry is an important trait for an educated person. If the ability to pay attention a desirable quality for an educated person then would the same be true for a civilized person? Are the abilities to critically listen, glean information, and reflect upon that information important virtues for a democratic society? Or would we prefer short attention spans, instant gratification, and surface learning?

My point about lecturing and paying attention is, I think, related to literacy. There seems to be a connection between effective lecturing, the ability to read, and the ability to pay attention. In his book *Why Johnny Can't Preach* T. David Gordon claims the traditional sermon is in decline because good preaching is in decline.[3] The television-weaned minister no longer reads deeply, especially literature and poetry, and therefore does not know how to construct a compelling sentence. Compounding the problem is the person in the pew who does not know how to pay attention to a sermon for more than five minutes. Wimpy reading produces wimpy preaching as well as wimpy listening. I imagine this disconnect exists in academia, business, and politics. But our inability to perform eloquently or pay attention closely is not a good reason to discard the sermon or the lecture. We should not retreat from lecturing because a student is bored or someone in the IT department tells us we have entered a new epoch that will not tolerate formal orality. To the contrary, we need to beef-up our efforts toward producing better public speakers and better listeners. Instructors need to work at making their lectures interesting and worthwhile. They also need to teach their students how to listen.

Lecturing is not the only method of communicating knowledge from the teacher to the pupil. The second is the tutorial system or the Socratic Method. The Socratic Method consists of asking questions for the purpose of either exposing the student's ignorance or pulling out from her some hidden truth. Highet says the tutorial system is the most difficult, the least used, but the most thorough way to teach.[4] It is easier to lecture to thirty students than it is to question three. It also takes less time to cover one hour's worth of lecture material than to extract the same information with relentless questioning. Typically, tutoring involves the student doing work on his own, then bringing it before the teacher for criticism and correction. The student then reflects upon the final product, comparing it to earlier attempts. Tutoring moves from pupil creation to teacher criticism to mutual appreciation.

While most public speaking instructors do not employ a pure Socratic Method, most utilize a modified one. Creativity, criticism, and appreciation are at the heart of what we do in my own public speaking classes. The student brings in a rough draft outline; I review it and make suggestions for improvement. The student prepares and delivers a speech, is evaluated, and then tries to improve with the next one.

Over the years I have made use of workshops where the student stands in front of the room and attempts to perform a short speech or a portion of one while I critique their efforts. For example, before my students do their

---

3. See Gordon, *Why Johnny Can't Preach*.

4. For Highet's explanation of tutoring, see *Art of Teaching*, 107–16.

demonstration speeches I have them perform their introductions. When a student finishes the first attempt I will have them repeat it with improvements. Sometimes I correct them in the middle of the exercise and require them to adjust at that moment: "Get your chin up. More volume. Don't laugh at yourself." Of course the other students are watching all of this and are secretly resolving not to make the same error before their turn comes around.

This sort of instruction—immediate, collective, and personal—cannot be efficiently replicated online. I suppose it *could* be replicated online, but the time and energy it would require would be self-defeating for the both the student and instructor.

The third method of communicating knowledge from the teacher to the pupil is preliminary work. Highet says preliminary work "assumes a written text, or a collection of documents, or a group of specimens, to be worth assimilating . . . and proceeds to explain its implications and test the pupil's comprehension of it."[5] In other words, some material in a course of study must be read, committed to memory, and tested. Reading assignments, quizzes, and exams usually fall into this category. In the case of public speaking it might also include students observing example speeches.

Highet is candid enough to say that he considers written tests and quizzes "horrible words."[6] He points out that when one considers the entire history of education, and what methods produced a well-educated person in the past, that higher examinations were most always oral. Since I happen to agree with Highet's assessment you will only find only one written exam in my public speaking course and perhaps two or three short written pop quizzes over the reading.

From these methods of communicating knowledge from teacher to pupil—lecturing, tutoring, and preliminary student work—one can see a prejudice toward orality. My point here is that public speaking has a long history of successfully being taught with an instructor and students communicating to each other, face-to-face, in a real time/space environment. Walter Ong has given us the term *secondary orality* by which he means various forms of communication, which make use of electronic media.[7] While there are similarities between primary and secondary orality, they should not be confused with each other. A person from our IT department once told me with the greatest sincerity that we should teach public

5. Ibid., 88.

6. Ibid., 118.

7. See Ong, *Orality and Literacy*, 11.

speaking online because that is the way young people communicate nowadays. However, what she failed to realized is that such a course would no longer be public speaking, but something else. Broadcasting maybe.

Not only does the teaching of public speaking have a prejudice toward orality, but the subject itself is a form of orality. The speaker, audience, and instructor monitor the components of volume, pitch, rate, stress, body language, posture, eye contact, facial expression, attire, and gestures. While an online course in public speaking might require students to visually record their speeches for instructor-delayed review, this practice poses several complications. First, it does not and cannot approximate an actual public speaking situation where verbal and nonverbal factors should be observed in an actual time/space situation. Second, the technical requirements for such an endeavor can be cumbersome for both the instructor and student. The quality of speeches may suffer because they are presented in unusual settings and may be poorly recorded making evaluation and feedback difficult. In-class preparatory activities like the ones described above would be extremely thorny to pull off. Third, since administrators justify online public speaking courses as being "more efficient" there is the tendency to pack as many students as possible in a class. This only raises the workload for the instructor, which in turn affects the overall quality of the course.

The way I now teach public speaking seems to be working well, and I therefore see no reason to change its mode of delivery from oral to electronic. Teaching public speaking online would only jeopardize the quality of the course. This is a purely practical matter, and should be sufficient in and of itself. However, there is another reason I am not going to teach public speaking online, one that involves how I see myself with students.

Vocational Concerns

The second major reason I am not going to teach public speaking online concerns my vocational calling. I prefer the term vocational calling to "job" or "career" because I think it implies a deeper purpose for work beyond receiving a monthly paycheck. Like many people, I suppose, my vocational calling was not made clear to me until I had reached adulthood and realized my particular inclinations and abilities. Yet, even as a child I imagined myself doing other things as a grownup. At five I wanted to be an archeologist and imagined myself digging up dinosaur bones. Sometime later I wanted to be a scuba diver and imagined myself beneath the water with dangerous sharks. At one point I wanted to be a broadcast journalist and imagined myself getting the "big scoop" on a story. My perceptions of teaching were formed not only from being a student but also from memories of my mother teaching first grade. My perceptions of teaching always involved a teacher in a classroom with students—a real physical space where face-to-face exchange occurred on a regular basis. So when I became a teacher I imagined being with students in a classroom. I did not imagine myself sitting in front of a computer screen by myself.

The point being made here is that my calling, or at least my perception of it, is to be with students. Of course there are other learning environments other than the classroom—the field, the workplace, the home. But even these spaces are shared with the teacher and student. When teachers are asked, as they increasingly will be, to spend their hours in front of a computer screen and not with actual students *incarnately* then they are being asked to do something that has seldom been understood as teaching. What online teaching proponents are really advocating is that we redefine what it means to be a teacher. Certainly there are those who would welcome a new model because they already spend a great deal of time in front of a computer screen. For example, people who say they are called to teach computer programming might actually prefer being in a room with a computer than being in a room with students. However, I must confess I do not feel this way. While there are times I need to be away from the students, the joy of my profession is found in their company. My calling is to be *with* them.

There is a joke that goes like this: I would love teaching were it not for the students. The joke has many derivatives: I would love being a doctor were it not for the patients. I would love being a minister were it not for the church members. I would love being a salesperson were it not for the customers. The joke would not be funny without the warrant that teachers, doctors, ministers, and salespeople are supposed to be with the people they serve. It is not only their calling, but their sacred duty. It may be too much to suggest that teachers must love their students, although there is nothing wrong with the idea. We are not afraid to say the teacher must love his or her subject. Not all doctors love their patients; nevertheless, they have a responsibility toward them which is made apparent when they stand next to the patient's bed, read the chart, pull up the chair, and converse over their condition. If this is not love, then it is something akin to it even if it is directed toward duty, and we are the better for it. We become uncomfortable when the doctor does not check on us or when we cannot find the salesperson. We want our minister to come see us when a loved one dies instead of emailing us words of sympathy.

I have a wicked suspicion that some online teachers might be trying to hide from their students. Teaching can be psychologically intimidating at times, especially in the early years when the waters are unfamiliar. What teacher has not wanted to run out of the room never to return at some time or another? These feelings usually, and hopefully, diminish over time and the teacher becomes comfortable with their students. However, if the teacher never has a desire to be with students—if they would prefer to escape their presence—then would it be unreasonable to suggest they may not be called to teach? If this proposition sounds too harsh, then those called to the profession should at least consider why they would prefer sitting in front of a computer screen and not standing in front of their students.

This leads us to the matter of inducement and the erroneous belief that technology is a neutral force; that the means of content delivery is somehow irrelevant. Why would a teacher so readily agree, assuming they are not forced by an ardent administration, to leave the classroom and sit in their office, never to physically see, hear, or smell, another student? It must have something to do with their high opinion of technology as a tool to solve problems. But technology is more than just a tool; it is also an *inducement*, something so strong most people are unable to refuse it.[8] Historian and rhetorician Richard Weaver pointed out how our technologies possess not only character but *being*. "Its simple being is a standing temptation to use it," says Weaver. "The fact that it is there seems to induce us to find additional opportunities for its use."[9] Since new technologies build upon old ones, the inducement is always toward the next upgrade with little thought given to the unintended consequences of advancement.

Not only is technology an inducement, but also the language that surrounds new technologies is *inducing*. The social theorist Jacques Ellul claimed the end of all modern propaganda is not understanding or acceptance but *compliance*, and this is especially true with the introduction of new technologies that mediate human communication and which tend to diminish traditional social groupings.[10] That is why Bell Telephone's slogan was so compelling years ago. Using the telephone was said to be "the next

---

8. See Wood, "Prime Time," 22.

9. Weaver, "Humanism," 68.

10. See Ellul, *Propaganda*, 90.

best thing to being there." But who ever asked, "Then what's the best thing?" The answer of course is "being there."

The American writer E. B. White warned us six decades ago that our technologies will come to insist that we forget the primary and near in favor of the secondary and the remote. White predicted that the day was coming when we would look into another person's face and see mere artifice.[11] Even before White's pronouncement, another writer, E. M. Forster, made a similar warning in his 1909 short story "The Machine Stops." In Forster's story people have no need to visit each other because human life is connected to a worldwide mechanical apparatus. The Machine brings images and voices into the underground rooms were individuals live so that there is little need to go outside or travel about or communicate face-to-face. The character of Vashti spends her days lecturing to an audience through an electronic plate on a variety of subjects ranging from the French Revolution to music during the Australian period. When her son Kuno, who lives on the other side of the earth, refuses to communicate his most intimate feelings through The Machine, he reaches out to Vashti.

"I want you to come and *see* me," he insists.

"I *can* see you," Vashti says through the plate, "What more do you want?"

The question implies that his mother actually preferred artifice over face-to-face interaction, that she really did not care to see him at all and that seeing his face in a machine was good enough—an unnatural and cold response if there ever was one.

The British economist E. F. Schumacher understood how cold statements like these could so easily be made in a society that had surrendered to the sovereignty of technology.[12] He once wrote, "The violence that is in the process of destroying the world is the cold, calculating, detached, heartless, and relentless violence that springs from over-extended minds working out of control of under-developed hearts."[13] Schumacher wrote in 1973 that economic growth had become an obsession to all modern societies so that even if the market produced something that was ugly, degrading, soul-destroying, or contrary to the well being of future generations, it really did not matter. As long as it can be shown to be economically beneficial then it should not be

11. White, "Removal," 2–3, as quoted in Slouka, *War of the Worlds*, 151–52.

12. This is Postman's definition of modern technological society as expounded in *Technopoly*.

13. Quoted in Pearce, *Small Is Still Beautiful*, 313.

questioned.[14] This sort of abstractionism does not see individual faces. It is only concerned with allotting resources and creating outlets.

At this juncture an objection might be raised. Suppose students actually preferred taking public speaking online? Would offering it to them then be justified? The problem with this line of reasoning is that there are some students who would prefer not to attend class at all and still receive credit for it. How many students if given the chance would vote to cancel their final exams every semester? How many of them think they deserve an "A" just because they show up for class? We would hope there would be few students like this, but the fact that there are students like this explains why diploma mills exist. Administrators should be careful about adopting a business model that says "the customer is always right." The customer, in this case the student, may not know or want what is in their best interest.

As far as I know, there is no research that would suggest that using a computer makes a person more intelligent or sociable. I suppose there is quite a bit of research that would suggest using a computer makes a person a better computer user and perhaps even a better global citizen, whatever that is. I am not aware of any research that would suggest using a computer makes one a better orator.

Lowell Monke, who worked with children and computers for two decades, claims in an *Orion* article, "Charlotte's Webpage: Why Children Shouldn't Have the World at Their Fingertips," that digital technology in the classroom is a Faustian bargain.[15] While computers might make children better global citizens, it also has the potential to alter their perceptions of reality and how they interact with the world. "I came to realize that the power of computers can lead children into deadened, alienated, and manipulative relationships with the world," Monke says, "that children's increasingly pervasive use of computers jeopardizes their ability to belong fully to human and biological communities—ultimately jeopardizing the communities themselves."[16]

Monke wonders if children who are immersed into a virtual world at an early age will be able to respect the actual world when they get older. Will they be able to draw a line between a sign on a screen and what the sign signifies? He says it is much easier to cut and paste a tree on a computer screen than it is to cut down one in the woods. However, the real

14. Schumacher, *Small Is Beautiful*, 27.

15. Monke, "Charlette's Webpage."

16. Ibid., 26.

world resists you. A person who grows up disconnected from the real world may not see the importance of taking care of real people or real places. Monke became disturbed when he noticed how entire groups of students would suddenly disappear from cyber-conversations related to their class projects. Relationships maintained electronically are much easier to sever when they become too demanding or intense. Children quickly learn that online relationships are easier to start, easier to control, and easier to quit in comparison to face-to-face relationships.

The abstractionists who call for more and more courses to be put online are not thinking about how digital technology degrades human relationships. They are not thinking about how teachers perceive their vocations as one of being with students in a real time/space environment. They are not thinking about the quality of education a student will receive. What they are thinking about are numbers, the bottom line, and efficiency. The more they continue to think this way the longer they will remain cold and heartless.

The Superiority of Embodied Teaching

The third major reason I am not going to teach public speaking online concerns the notion of embodiment to which I have already alluded. This last reason will perhaps be less convincing to a portion of my audience because it contains a certain philosophical bias expressed in the Christian religion. Nevertheless, I do not apologize for it because as a Christian I simply cannot lay aside my core beliefs toward the world and assume a position of objective neutrality anymore than a die-hard materialist can do so. As Jacques Ellul has pointed out, the conscientious Christian "cannot help thinking in theological terms, because his vocation as an intellectual impels him to think out his faith."[17]

Despite this philosophical bias, I am inclined to think some non-Christians will agree with some of what I have to say about embodiment. Conversely, some Christians may disagree with me on this point as they have tended to do so in the past under the influence of Gnosticism, a philosophy that teaches the body is evil. Orthodox Christianity holds that God the Father must have felt embodiment was important, otherwise he would not have sent his Son in the flesh: "That which was from the beginning, which we have heard, which we have seen with our eyes, which we looked upon and have touched with our hands, concerning the word of life—the

17. Ellul, *Presence of the Kingdom*, 96.

life was made manifest, and we have seen it, and testify to it and proclaim to you the eternal life, which was with the Father and was made manifest to us—"[18] For many Christians the doctrine of the incarnation reveals how real presence is a requirement for real love. That is to say, earthly embodiment was a necessary element of Christ's self-identification with human beings in procuring salvation for his people. If we extend this notion one step further, we might say our love toward others necessitates real presence if we are going to be Christ-like.

Wendell Berry draws a comparison between the old dualism as expressed in Gnosticism and the current degradation and obsolescence of the body found in modern "technological progress."[19] He says the new dualism is more destructive than ever as more and more people look "upon the body, along with the rest of the natural creation, as intolerably imperfect by mechanical standards."[20] Armed with computers the new Gnostics see the body as an encumbrance of the mind—"the mind, that is, as reduced to a set of mechanical ideas that can be implemented in machines—and so they hate it and long to be free of it."[21] Berry refuses to use a computer when he engages in writing because he does not want to diminish or distort his bodily involvement in work. At first glance his reasoning seems inapplicable to writing, something Neil Postman observed as a symbol system of a symbol system, twice removed from reality.[22] Dancing, gardening, or carpentry seem more like arts of the body than writing, but Berry explains that language is the most intimately physical of all the artistic means:

> We have it palpably in our mouths; it is our *langue*, our tongue. Writing it, we shape it with our hands. Reading aloud what we have written—as we must do, if we are writing carefully—our language passes in at the eyes, out at the mouth, in at the ears; the words are immersed and steeped in the senses of the body before they make sense to the mind. They cannot make sense in the mind until they have made sense in the body.[23]

Berry's observation shows writing as an extension of orality, thus, its dependency on the body. How much more, then, is public speaking an art

18. 1 John 1:1–2 ESV.

19. See Berry, "Feminism," 178–96.

20. Ibid., 191.

21. Ibid.

22. See Postman and Paglia, "She Wants Her TV," 45.

23. Berry, "Feminism," 192.

of the body? In watching the popular movie *The King's Speech* one is impressed at how the king's tutor, Lionel Logue, immersed his majesty into bodily awareness for the purpose of correcting his speech impediment. Logue's techniques exercised the whole body—legs, arms, back, chest, head, jaw, teeth, and tongue. I seriously doubt if the king's lisp could have been cured with an online course. The situation necessitated real presence and embodied teaching.

Embodied teaching is superior to disembodied teaching because students need to know what the right thing looks like. Without an incarnate model to follow, they do not know what to do.[24] I would like to think this is why Jesus called his disciples to himself for three years and why Dietrich Bonhoeffer founded a seminary based on a "life together" with his ordinands.[25] The principle here is the same principle that accompanies good parenting. "Kindness" is only an abstraction until modeled. Sally must see her father show kindness to her mother so she can imitate it. Likewise, the public speaking student benefits from seeing the teacher demonstrate proper posture and effective eye contact. She benefits from having the teacher stand in front of her saying, "Now do as I do." Abstractions or principles must be affirmed through imitation. Through repeated imitation comes understanding, and with understanding comes internalization.[26] Perhaps teachers within the arts best understand the importance of imitation. The student becomes like the master as they prepare for the concert hall or their own art show. In the same way, before industrialization fragmented the production process, one became a craftsman through an apprenticeship. Here the student and master held a special relationship as they shared the same work environment.

I realize how extremely difficult it is to justify a master-student relationship under an industrialized educational system, but I am convinced that its absence, despite the fact that more people are being formally educated, has contributed to a decline in real learning. The desire to "get as many people through" using the most "efficient means" is symptomatic of a technological society unable to establish meaningful significance outside of a technological solution. Thus, online public speaking is suggested in dean meetings with little blush, little sense of irony. "Seeing no other source of

24. See Wilson, "Educating the Imagination," 160.
25. See Metaxas, *Bonhoeffer*, 266–73.
26. Wilson, "Educating the Imagination," 160.

security, and failing to recognize the illusoriness of their technical freedom, they become slaves to the exacting determinations of efficiency."[27]

Conclusion

I am not going to teach public speaking online because my current mode of delivery works extremely well, my calling demands that I be with the students in person, and I believe embodied teaching is superior to disembodied teaching.

I would venture that I am not the only university professor, let alone teacher of public speaking, who feels this way. Due to the push for online courses and programs, it would be in the interest of higher education for administrators, faculty, IT specialists, and online departments to have a frank discussion over the following questions. What is at stake is the very notion of teaching itself and whether our students will receive a worthwhile education.

Should our university place a limit (or percentage) to the number of online courses and degree programs it offers?

How does the increase of online courses and programs alter the essential nature of our university? How does it change our sense of place, traditional classroom learning, and job security for faculty?

Are the qualities, skills, and knowledge desired in a traditional classroom instructor the same for an online instructor? Why or why not?

Should an online instructor be "forced" to teach an online course, especially if they were hired to teach in a traditional classroom environment?

Are there some courses, which do not translate well to an online equivalent? If so, what kind of courses would they be (e.g., sculpting, tennis, acting, public speaking, first aid, etc.)

Ultimately, who will control the creation and growth of online courses and programs at our university—the administration, the faculty, the online program department?

Who will monitor the quality and effectiveness of online courses and programs in relation to student learning?

27. Christians, "Ellul," 125.

5

Progress

What Happens When We Get Too Big for Our Britches

If you are on the wrong road, progress means doing an about-turn and walking back to the right road; and in that case the man who turns back soonest is the most progressive man.

—C. S. LEWIS[1]

THE IDEA THAT HUMANS are progressing in a definite and desirable direction was generally unknown until the Enlightenment.[2] Moral progress was known of course—classical antiquity spoke of the reciprocal patterns of birth, growth, decline, and decadence—but not the *continuous material improvement of life on earth*. Ancient pagan societies were not even able to develop the basic rudiments of science because they either viewed the world as chaotic or in pantheistic terms. To poke and prod nature would mean disturbing the gods. The Hebrews and the early Christians had no notion of progress as we do today. Christianity speaks of creation, fall, redemption, and consummation, but nothing of the idea of man progressively moving in a definite and desirable direction. Postmillennialism, a minority view in Protestant eschatology, teaches movement towards social betterment, but this progression depends on the advancement of the gospel and the work of the Holy Spirit, and it does not deny man's innate depravity. Aspects of modern liberalism often cloaks itself with Christian rhetoric to advance

1. Lewis, *Mere Christianity*, 28.
2. This is the assertion made by Bury in *Idea of Progress*.

policies that confirm the modern notion of progress, but these efforts are largely vacant of any insistence that sin is spiritually fatal or that conversion is necessary.

Christianity as a whole has always viewed life in this world as a sojourn with greater hope anticipated in the life hereafter. Yet Christians are in the world, and the message of the cross presupposes the world cannot be left alone. The notable feature about American Manifest Destiny is how it infused the gospel with a broader cultural mandate to conquer physical space so that its purposes were not merely spiritual and persuasive, but geographic and civic as well. If the Puritans had not believed the wilderness could yield to their directives they probably would not have had the wherewithal to survive. The Old Testament narrative of subduing a Promised Land was not only convenient for them, but highly functional as well.

The First Amendment terminated any hope of a Puritan state, but it did nothing to douse the inherent functionalism found among New England colonists once their faith yielded to the tenets of the Enlightenment. As early as the seventeenth century, Harvard had assigned *technologia* as the successor of metaphysics. No problem existed which could not be settled by method.[3] We would do well to remember that functionalism was the lubricant of the Industrial Revolution. As Richard Weaver says, "The impulse to domineer over creation and certain habits of concentrating interest were due to serve the future institutions of business and science."[4]

The Modern Notion of Progress

The modern notion of progress began with Bacon, Newton, and Locke, and with the declaration that scientific technique can provide us the expectation of continuous material and social improvement. Bacon and Newton suggested that if we observe Nature closely enough she would divulge her secrets to us—God's secrets—to be harnessed for our benefit. Under the liberal capitalist paradigm the exploitation of earth's resources and human labor became justifiable. As discoveries in natural science increased, so did the number of technical innovations and the scale whereby they were utilized. The land-based economy was disrupted and eventually overturned. With industrialism came centralization, population shifts, urbanization, wealth concentration, and economic instability. In analyzing the culminating effects of industrialism

3. See McLuhan's discussion of the New England mind in "Southern Quality," 367.

4. Weaver, "Two Diarists," 746.

at the onset of the Great Depression, Lyle H. Lanier observed, "The stream of goods from the machines, the drive for ever-increasing production and consumption, and the generally accelerated tempo of social change served to popularize the doctrine of progress."[5]

The modern notion of progress assumes advancement will continue indefinitely, that, as J. B. Bury says in *The Idea of Progress*, it is the earth's great business that "a condition of general happiness will ultimately be enjoyed, which will justify the whole process of civilization." Progress is not predicated on any external will, says Bury, but on man's ability, otherwise, "there would be no guarantee of its continuance . . . and the idea of Progress would lapse into the idea of Providence."[6] Under this definition, progress is man taking the steering wheel away from God and going at it alone.

And this is the great danger of progressivism—going at it alone as if God was not there or did not care. The modern notion of progress abandons moral discourse for technological know-how. It becomes impossible to question technological innovation from a moral or ethical stance when we believe civilization is constantly advancing. Jacques Ellul referred to this circumstance as the Technological Bluff.[7] Our increasing dependence on technology diverts us so that we do not consider its consequences. If someone raises an objection to an innovation—where it might take us or what it might do to us—the progressive quickly renounces him or her with one little sentence: "But technological change is inevitable." No one could have ever uttered such a statement before Bacon. Under these circumstances inevitability is elevated to a virtue, and its newly established ethos becomes a marketing strategy. Ultimately, the doctrine of inevitability determines by fiat what might otherwise be open for discussion.[8]

The modern notion of progress is joined at the hip to liberal capitalist democracy and its current stage of hyper-consumption. Again, Lanier says, "Progress is perhaps the most widely advertised commodity offered for general consumption, a sort of universal social enzyme whose presence is essentially to the ready assimilation of other commodities, material and intellectual, generated by the machine age."[9] In this way progress becomes both a slogan and a philosophy, "a device for social control and belief in the reality of

5. Lanier, "Critique of the Philosophy of Progress," 132.

6. Bury, *Idea of Progress*, 5.

7. See Ellul, *Technological Bluff*.

8. See Slouka, *War of the Worlds*, 143.

9. Lanier, "Critique of the Philosophy of Progress," 123.

a process of cosmic development toward 'some far-off divine event."[10] Progress never defines its ultimate objective but "thrusts its victims at once into an infinite series," writes John Crowe Ransom in *I'll Take My Stand*. "Our progressives are the latest version of those pioneers who conquered the wilderness, except that they are pioneering on principle, or from force of habit, and without any recollection of what pioneering was for."[11]

The question, "Why do we create things?" is obscured when progress has no clear end in sight. The reasoning behind technological innovation becomes circular: "We create things because we *can* create things." But we can no longer afford this kind of thinking—that is, thinking without moral clarification—because our survival is at stake, and "progress" now has the capacity to jerk us back to the Dark Ages. Just because we *can* do a thing, does not mean that we *should* do a thing.

Lewis Mumford, no stranger to the society-altering capabilities of technology, writes, "However far modern science and technics have fallen short of their inherent possibilities, they have taught mankind at least one lesson: Nothing is impossible." Technological society is not just the next stage of industrialism; it is a new way of human living never fully anticipated by pre-moderns. How should we live if *nothing* is impossible?[12] That is to say, what does it mean for humanity if we define our purpose of living as being a satisfied customer (the ethos of consumer economics) or alter what it means to be human itself (the direction of biotechnology) or perhaps even destroy ourselves altogether (through weapons of mass destruction)?

The Abolition of Man

In his classic work *The Abolition of Man* C. S. Lewis warns us that man's conquest of nature could turn out to be nature's conquest of man. Powerful technologies, plus the absence of traditional and universal morality (what Lewis calls the Tao), plus the willingness to use these technologies over people, will produce the demise of man.[13] Lewis argues that the problem in the past had always been how to transfer wisdom from one generation to the next, or what he referred to as old birds teaching young birds how to fly.

10. Ibid., 122.

11. Ransom, "Reconstructed but Unregenerate," 8.

12. For a fuller treatment of this question, see Jardine, *Making and Unmaking of Technological Society*.

13. See Lewis, *Abolition of Man*.

Up until now, the old exchange involved "conforming the soul to reality," accomplished through the passing on of knowledge, self-discipline, and virtue. But we have moved from the transmission of wisdom to something never practiced before in the history of our existence—the transforming of the species altogether.

Equipped with a magical bag of charms, the new Conditioners will manipulate people for their own good pleasure. "The man-moulders of the new age will be armed with the powers of an omnicompetent state and an irresistible scientific technique," says Lewis, "We shall get at last a race of conditioners who really cut out all posterity in what shape they please."[14] Lewis mentions the technologies of mass media, contraception, and genetic engineering as examples of humankind's new found power over nature. The Conditioners will substitute the material values of food, drink, sex, amusement, science, long life, and the like, in place of a higher good.

The power to manipulate people through technique for self-seeking ends is the twin, the same motivation, of the medieval enchanter. The magical endeavor and the scientific endeavor are the same, only the latter can now actually deliver the goods. Lewis points out that in bargaining with the devil, Faust did not really want knowledge, but gold, guns, and girls. The abolition of man is the "process whereby man surrenders object after object, and finally himself, to Nature in return for power."[15] The Conditioners will not care about the conditioned; in fact, they will hate them. Without moral restraint provided by the Tao, the Conditioners will do whatever they want. They will not act out of any sense of duty or common good. This is precisely the point George Orwell was trying to make in the novel *1984*. O'Brien tells Winston while torturing him, "The Party seeks power entirely for its own sake. We are not interested in the good of others; we are interested solely in power." "If you want a picture of the future," he says, "imagine a boot stamping on a human face—forever."

Orwell gave us a picture of tyranny with a sad face, but totalitarianism can wear a happy face as well. Aldous Huxley imagined the most efficient totalitarian state would be one where people did not have to be coerced into obedience because they loved their servitude. Huxley anticipated that having the technological means to blow the world up several times over would insure a perpetual militarism among governments unless some other technological solution was offered. The proposition of *Brave New World*

14. Ibid., 73.
15. Ibid., 67.

is that if the world was given a choice between annihilation and stability, it would choose stability, even if the stability meant a radical revolution in human minds and bodies. In Huxley's novel, compliance is secured through conditioning the population from birth so that meaning in life is found in consumption and pleasure. Therefore, in *Brave New World* humans are hatched from test tubes rather than born from the womb; there are no mothers and fathers, only conditioning centers; everyone is promiscuous; everyone is a happy shopper; joy is found in the latest novelty, whether it's the newest feelie (movie) or the most recent glitzy gadget. Life, in short, is a perpetual round of entertainments. The citizens do not question their shallow lives because history has been erased from their memory, and they cannot remember the former world.

The point being made here is this: whether we end up with a totalitarian state with a sad face or one with a happy face, it doesn't matter because both involve the loss of the Tao—and consequently our humanity—through conditioning.

The power to manipulate nature, if turned on man, ends in tragedy, for those who exercise such power over their subjects will end up destroying themselves in the process. Because while the Conditioners reject the Tao, they are still subject to their own selfish impulses, and the Conditioned are subject to their own selfish impulses as well, even while having the Tao conditioned out of them. If Man destroys man, then Nature is still left standing and laughs at the whole ordeal. "Man's conquest of Nature turns out, in the moment of its consummation, to be Nature's conquest of Man," says Lewis. "We thought we were beating her back when she was luring us on. What looked to us like hands held up in surrender was really the opening arms to enfold us for ever."[16] Thus, Nature is troubled with us no more, and there will be no one there to speak any longer of truth, mercy, beauty, or happiness.

This is the abolition of man. The Conditioners cannot act upon their subjects without acting upon themselves. To use another human being as you would a block of wood diminishes both maker and the one made. The one who stands to profit and the one who has been cut to order are one and the same. Our soul belongs to the devil, metaphorically speaking, because having denied the Tao and having attempted to change our own natures, the power unleashed no longer belongs to us. We are slaves to the thing to which we have given ourselves. "If man chooses to treat himself as raw

16. Ibid., 80.

material, raw material he will be: not raw material to be manipulated, as he fondly imagined, by himself, but by mere appetite, that is, mere Nature, in the person of his dehumanized Conditioners."[17]

Getting Back on the Right Path

If a nuclear war were to destroy civilization as we know it, there would still be the prospect of never completely losing the technical knowledge that killed us in the first place. This is one of the major themes in Walter Miller's novel *A Canticle for Leibowitz*. Over the centuries the post-apocalyptic monks of the Albertian Order of Leibowitz preserved scientific knowledge, but they could not prevent that knowledge from slipping through their fingers, even after a nuclear holocaust. The motif of recurrence in Miller's novel suggests that once a certain technology is hatched there is little chance it will ever be completely eradicated, even if buried under centuries of rubble. We must therefore learn to live with our technologies. The automobile—that wondrous invention that awarded us the family motor vacation and at the same time severed community and family ties—will remain with us in some form. Electricity is not going away any time soon. This is not entirely bad. Technological staying power has its benefits, especially when one considers the performance of penicillin or sewage treatment plants. Nevertheless, there is a cumulative effect of technological reliance, especially in relation to increasing scale and when no thought is given to unintended consequences. We are therefore left with negotiating and appropriating our new technologies. The goal is not to loath technology, but to properly appropriate it for the quality of life we seek.

What we should be striving for is a synthesis between a sane past and a hysterical future. What should be seeking is some degree of *balance*. Confucius said, "Balance is one of the basis of the world; harmony is the universal and permanent law."[18] The principle of balance is found in many disciplines, philosophies, and religions. Aristotle's Golden Mean teaches that moral virtue is the middle ground between two extremes. Likewise, the Middle Way associated with Buddhism sets its adherents on a path of moderation that avoids the extremes of sensual indulgence on one hand

17. Ibid., 84.

18. Confucius, *Chung-Yung*, chapter 1, quoted in Fletcher, "Education, Past and Present," 92–93.

and self-denial on the other. Christianity has its own version of balance as it holds out the virtue of moderation or self-control.

To speak of balance is to speak *ecologically*, a term derived from the Greek word *oikos* meaning household. Aristotle insisted that a harmonious home was one where all members worked together to benefit the whole. The principle of balance is foundational to biological ecology, a field that considers the relationships between life forms and their environments. Ecology views life holistically. Starting with individual organisms, it moves out to populations (individuals of the same species), and then on to communities. An ecosystem is comprised of a community of populations together with its physical environment. Ecological rings of study start with the cell and then move out to the organ, to the organism, to the population, to the community, to the immediate environment, and finally to the larger region. Questions that concern ecologists include: To what extent does competition for food determine which species can coexist in a habitat? What role does disease play in the dynamics of populations? What is the relationship between soil productivity and plant community structure? What are some species more vulnerable to extinction than others?[19]

Ecologists first look for patterns within systems to explain what exactly is occurring. Once patterns are discerned they are capable of predicting what could happen to a population under a particular set of circumstances. If the circumstances are potentially harmful, then intervention might be warranted to preserve the ecosystem. Ecology, then, becomes pro-active when it attempts to control plagues, exploit crops, or save a species. These are deliberate adjustments taken to restore ecological balance.

Modern ecology is often associated with the nineteenth-century German biologist Ernst Haeckel, who as a zoologist, naturalist, philosopher, physician, professor, and artist looked at the living world from many different vantage points. Ecological practices, however, predate Haeckel by hundreds, even thousands of years. When the earliest colonists arrived on America's shores, they saw how the Indians burned forests to create hunting grounds, planted corn and other vegetables, and followed the food wherever it might be seasonally available. Native Americans *used* the land but did *use it up* as the white settlers were prone to do. The Indians could always find more beaver and buffalo, but new Americans almost trapped and shot these species out of existence.

19. Townsend et al., *Essentials of Ecology*, 6.

Early farmers were ecologists by necessity because they had to understand the growth and retardation of animal populations and harness this knowledge to their benefit. They had to know how to maximize food collection from the natural environment over extended periods of time, use domesticated plants and animals for best rates of return, and protect their food from natural enemies such as pathogens and parasites.[20]

I belong to an academic fellowship called the Media Ecology Association. A sub-field of communication studies, the association has intentionally borrowed its name from the biological sciences to suggest there is a relationship between media and human beings, which contributes to the formation of culture. The late Neil Postman defined media ecology as a subject that "looks into the matter of how media of communication affect human perception, understanding, feeling, value, and how our interaction with media facilitates or impedes our chances of survival."[21] Postman believed media ecology should ask serious questions about humanity's relationship to new technologies, especially communication technologies. These questions include: To what extent does a particular technology contribute to the use of rational thought? To what degree does a particular technology contribute to the development of democratic processes? To what extent does a particular technology contribute to greater access to *meaningful* information? To what degree does a new technology enhance or diminish our moral sense, our capacity for goodness?[22]

Questions like these assume it is possible for a culture to lose control of its symbolic balance. And when this happens, as Postman insisted, an adjustment is in order. In the same way a person would adjust a thermostat in a room if he or she were feeling too warm or too cool, awakened elements in a culture must not be afraid to get up off their metaphorical couches and act when they sense something is wrong. Postman believed educational institutions were best qualified to be cultural-thermostat-adjusters, and this for him made teaching a conserving activity.[23] In the late 1970s Postman wrote:

> Our own culture is overdosing on change. One may call it "future shock," "culture shock," "technology shock," or whatever. The plain fact is that too much change, too fast, for too long has the effect of making social institutions useless and individuals perpetually unfit

20. Ibid., 5.

21. Postman, "What Is Media Ecology?"

22. See Postman, "Humanism of Media Ecology."

23. This is Postman's thesis in *Teaching as a Conserving Activity*.

to live amid the conditions of their own culture. . . . It is enough to say that we have reached the point where the problem of conservation, not growth, must now be solved. We know very well how to change but we have lost the arts of preservation. Without at least a reminiscence of continuity and tradition, without a place to stand from which to observe change, without a counterargument to the overwhelming thesis of change, we can easily be swept away—in fact, are being swept away.[24]

One may not agree with Postman that schools qualify as the best thermostat-adjusters, but his point that we have reached a place of a cultural imbalance is crucial in addressing our predicament. If we are going to survive Technopolis it will mean cultivating a counterargument to the modern notion of progress. The counterargument must not only describe the problem but also point to a way out.

There is much talk of grass roots movements these days. More of us are beginning to realize that our political and economic systems are so dysfunctional that any change to the status quo will have to start on the ground floor and work its way up and out. Toward the end of his life Paul Weyrich, cofounder of the Heritage Foundation, wrote, "The next conservative economics needs to define free enterprise more broadly, looking not just at the danger from government but also at the threat from vast corporations, many of them multi-nationals that could care less about America's future."[25] Weyrich recognized that conservatives have traditionally favored things local and small in scale, what Edmund Burke identified as "little platoons."

Finding our way back—or *out*—will, I believe, involve returning political and economic power back to families, communities, and local entities. This is the thing that will ward off our own growing mass of Conditioners. Ultimately, finding the correct path again means denying that the purpose in life is continuous material improvement—that we were put here for a reason beyond our own self-interest. To assert that we are God's creatures in a finite world that has a perceivable moral order is the ultimate mark of progress.

24. Ibid., 21.
25. Weyrich, "Next Conservative Economics," para. 4.

6

What's a Person to Do?

Work Beyond the Yellow Brick Road

I should have stayed on the farm. I should have listened to my old man. . . . You can't plant me in your penthouse. I'm going back to my plough.

—ELTON JOHN[1]

I REALLY DON'T KNOW if Elton John is the agrarian type. His jewel-studded glasses and flamboyant personae would seem to indicate otherwise, yet, his song, "Goodbye Yellow Brick Road," strangely captures a certain sentiment toward rural life, and for the purposes of this essay the lyrics might be construed to describe our troublesome economic times:

When are you gonna come down?

When are you going to land?

Economists have said the recovery is going to be slower than expected. Some say we will never regain the jobs that have been lost. Politicians on both sides of the aisle say we need to retrain ourselves for what's coming—that is, if they even know what's coming. At the university where I teach the slogan being constantly drummed into the mind is that we must prepare our students to compete in the global marketplace.

However, of late my confidence in the global marketplace has been waning. The tendency is to assume the current recession is merely a correction within the familiar boom and bust cycles of modern capitalism.

1. Elton John, "Goodbye Yellow Brick Road," on *Greatest Hits*, This Compilation, This Record Co., Recorded 1974.

American presidents come to us explaining what they will do to "fix" the broken economy. The interventions they suggest are more frequent and require greater measures. How does anyone begin to fix a national debt of seventeen trillion? The Emerald City seems to have lost its luster. The promises once associated with the yellow brick road are fading fast.

Where Did All the Jobs Go?

Between 2009 and 2011 the unemployment rate hovered above 9 percent.[2] Current unemployment figures do not take into account those who have stopped looking for work or those who have taken lower paying jobs to keep their houses. Taken together, the unemployed, the underemployed, and those who have abandoned the work force total perhaps 15 percent of the labor market. Ironically, U.S. companies are raking in more profits now than before the recession, and they are doing this by unburdening themselves of American workers and hiring cheaper labor in China, India, and Brazil.

If you haven't lost your job yet, you probably have seen a decline in your real income. *USA Today* recently reported that every generation born after 1955 has been sinking economically.[3] According to the Census Bureau my own gender-age grouping (men 45–54) suffered an 11.2 percent decline in median income from 2000–2008.[4] The median wage in this country has not grown in thirty years. Despite what anyone says about growth economics, the United States is not prospering from it, and neither are many other countries around the globe.

Princeton economics professor Alan S. Blinder created no small stir five years ago with the publication of "Offshoring: The Next Industrial Revolution?" in *Foreign Affairs*.[5] The piece predicted outsourcing overseas will go beyond manufacturing jobs and extend into the service economy. Blinder reminds us that in the first Industrial Revolution farmers left their households and plots of land to work in the factory. Ninety percent of work was to be found on the farm in 1810 compared to only 3 percent in manufacturing. By 1960, 25 percent of all American jobs were in manufacturing compared to only 8 percent in agriculture. Today there are fewer than two million farmers in America. More people are incarcerated than farm. The

2. U.S. Department of Labor, "Unemployment," n.p.

3. *USA Today*, "Incomes."

4. Ibid.

5. See Binder, "Offshoring."

second Industrial Revolution shifted work away from manufacturing and toward services. Under the second Industrial Revolution we saw the malling of America and the arrival of the big box distribution stores.

Blinder says we are now in the midst of a third Industrial Revolution—what some have called the information-service economy. While the second Industrial Revolution marked the outsourcing of American blue-collar jobs, the third Industrial Revolution marks the outsourcing of many white-collar professional service jobs. Any work that can be delivered through a wire is vulnerable. Most physicians have nothing to worry about, but radiologists do. Police officers seem safe for now, but security guards can be replaced with electronic monitoring systems. Janitors and plumbers are immune, but not accountants and computer programmers. If courses in higher education can so easily be taught online, then college professors can expect their jobs to be at risk as well. Not all personal services can be transmitted electronically, but as technology continues to advance, more personal services will be up for grabs.

In the midst of all this volatility comes the educator and the government official telling us that no child should be left behind and that everyone should go to college because what the new information economy demands is "knowledge workers." The rhetoric is downright scolding and essentially boils down to this: "Get smart or be a loser" or "If you don't have a college degree you're future is most certainly doomed." Policymakers scold us when they sense we are not doing enough to speed up their vision of progress. There is nothing new in this. Secretary of Agriculture Earl Butz scolded the American farmer in the 1970s when he said, "Get big or get out." George W. Bush scolded us soon after the Twin Towers fell down when he said, "Go out and shop!" These are little prods that help keep consumerism on track. Our rate of consumption must not only stay on track; it must also increase from what it was last year, and it must be greater next year, and even greater the year after that. This is called economic wisdom.

But if we all go to college and become knowledge workers, then who will fix our cars and build our houses?[6] Our view of vocation seems to be little more than getting a certificate to get a job to enter a certain income bracket so we can buy more stuff. I am inclined to agree with social historian Christopher Lasch who said the university had evolved into a trade school

6. For a discussion of the perplexities of "knowledge workers," see Crawford, *Shop Class as Soulcraft*, 1–3.

for overgrown adolescents.[7] Lasch's vision for education reform included Jefferson's assumption that all citizens need a basic education, but higher education should only be available to those who were inclined to it.[8] As to the argument that we are falling behind in math and science in comparison to other industrial countries perhaps we need to ask, "What is the finish line we are all running toward anyway, the burning up of the world?"[9] We are like Dorothy and her companions in the *Wizard of Oz*, who arrive at the Great Green City with great expectations and unrealized dreams only to discover a crazed man behind a curtain pumping levers. "Pay no attention to that man!"

Darwinian Global Economics

The problem with modern economics—besides the fact that modern economists were unable to predict our current economic crisis—is that it has divorced itself from morality, local communities, and the natural family. Neoclassical economic theory is a science in much the same way chemistry is a science, given to physical measurement and mathematical formulas. Man is reduced to a machine cog when economics becomes mere technique. And if a machine part, then subject to tinkering, manipulation, and replacement by those who pull the levers. The study of economics would better be housed in the humanities, or better yet philosophy or theology, where it could ponder what people and families are for.

Industrialism brought an end to the family as an *economic* unit in Western society. First, the fathers went off to work in the factory. Then, the mothers started entering the workforce beginning with the Second World War. Finally, the care of the children was outsourced to various surrogate institutions. What was once provided by a home economy—education, health care, child rearing, and care of the elderly—became provided by the state. The rest of our needs—food, clothing, shelter, and entertainment—became provided by the corporations. The home is now the center of *consumption* rather than *production*. The great majority of us are hired hands who work for somebody else.

This new economic arrangement is called *progress* in much the same way Darwinian evolution is called progress. Darwinian global economics

7. See Miller, *Hope in a Scattering Time*, 173.

8. Ibid., 167.

9. Actually, this is Lasch's phrase. See Miller's mentioning of it in ibid., 337.

allows corporations to distance themselves from their long-standing social contract with employees, families, and local communities. In 1886, the Supreme Court arbitrarily gave corporations real person status, and over time this has lent credence to a dog-eat-dog individualism of the most extreme sort, so that "corporate individuals" feel little obligation to love their neighbors or act with moral restraint. Of late, Darwinian global economics has given us longer hours and lower wages in addition to job insecurity. Survival of the fittest means selling cheaply by using the cheapest labor possible, and that means pulling up the stakes and moving south or overseas when pressed with the notion of providing a living wage. In *The Corporation: The Pathological Pursuit of Profit and Power* Joel Bakan shows how corporations share the same traits of a sociopath—callous unconcern for the feelings of others, incapable of maintaining enduring relationships, reckless disregard for the safety of others, repeated lying and conning others for the sake of profit, an incapacity to experience guilt, and failure to conform to the social norms with respect to lawful behavior.[10]

There is little shame in all of this. The CEO of Mellon Bank, Robert Kelly, seamlessly equates capitalism with Darwinism. During the banking crisis he uttered to a PBS news anchor, "Capitalism works. Darwinism works." Kelly's comment is reminiscent of Michael Douglas' famous line in *Wall Street*: "Greed is right. Greed works." It is surprising how closely fervent capitalists have aligned themselves with the social Darwinists. What is even more surprising is the loyalty survival of the fittest economics receives from "conservative" Christians. Historically, Christians have been adversaries of the social Darwinists. At least they were when they rallied around William Jennings Bryan who fought to keep Darwinism out of the public schools in Tennessee. Bryan was not only repulsed by the thought of humans evolving from apes, but equally concerned with where Darwinism might lead in society at large. We must remember Bryan waged his attack from the political left, from the side of social reform, and that he was a pacifist who, like Albert Einstein, attributed the excesses of the Great War with the influence of Friedrich Nietzsche, perhaps our best known social Darwinist.[11]

10. Bakan, *Corporation*.

11. These perceptive insights on the link between social Darwinism and modern economics are derived from Robinson, "Darwinism," 28–75.

Consumed!

In his book *The Making and Unmaking of Technological Society* Murray Jardine traces liberal capitalist democracy through three stages: classical liberalism, reform liberalism, and neoclassical liberalism.[12] The first stage sought to secure liberty through constitutional government, a free-market economy, private property rights, and religious tolerance. The goal of classical liberalism was to maximize individual freedom by establishing a neutral system that did not privilege any particular social group. The objective was not to impose any way of life or belief upon individuals but to ensure basic individual rights. Far from being a neutral, however, classical liberalism favored the rising Protestant middle class, a segment of society that embraced wealth creation through hard work, thrift, and self-denial. This formula worked well for awhile and certainly raised levels of wealth, increased life expectancy, and gave us new won freedoms in the face of arbitrary powers, but classical liberalism also possessed a one-dimensional focus on material things, a fixation on wealth creation that far exceeded what humans actually needed. It was a materialistic bias that largely ignored spiritual and aesthetic values.

Classical liberalism seemed to have triumphed by the end of the nineteenth century; then came the twentieth century and World War I, the Russian Revolution, the Great Depression, and World War II. Reform liberalism was a reaction to the failures associated with classical liberalism, namely, the tendency of wealth and power to be concentrated in monopolies and capitalism's propensity for boom and bust cycles. Whereas classical liberalism viewed government as a threat to individual freedom, reform liberals like Franklin D. Roosevelt saw government as a stabilizing force. Even before the New Deal, British writer and historian Hilaire Belloc claimed capitalism was an unstable force and in conflict with the moral theories of liberty. Belloc pointed out that if *pure* capitalism reigned, people would be constantly unemployed, starving in the streets, and waging rebellion against the captains of industry. Ironically, monopolistic capitalism had to be undergirded by non-capitalist methods to ensure its stability. This is why the expansion of government power in the twentieth century coincided with the expansion of corporate power. Neither classical liberalism nor reform liberalism established a system of neutrality because

12. Much of this section on the three stages of liberal capitalist democracy is based upon Jardine, *Making and Unmaking of Technological Society*.

one favored the bourgeois class and the other favored managers and professionals—the "experts" needed to make a growing technocracy run more efficiently. Furthermore, reform liberalism only made the contradictions of classical liberalism more pronounced under its doctrine of "neutrality," which came to be translated as "no morality."

Reform liberalism held sway in America for several decades until it faced a series of challenges in the 1960s and 1970s. Among these was a less-than-successful military campaign in Vietnam, a growing alienation between World War II generation parents and their children, and a general increase of permissiveness and secularization in the culture. These challenges were followed by an economic downturn and high inflation during the Carter years. Reaganism and Thatcherism were attempts to resurrect classical liberalism. Jardine says the neoclassical liberalism of the postindustrial economy contained two major postulates: a return to laissez-faire economics and a revival of Protestant morality to counteract the growing moral permissiveness. However, in this new version of laissez-faireism, the market became a model for everything, and individual choice was deified, which had the unintended consequence of extinguishing the old Protestant work ethic. One cannot be thrifty and overindulgent at the same time.

In a consumer culture, corporations must *create* demand, and this is done primarily through an all-pervasive environment of advertising and through material immediacy associated with extended credit. Adam Smith assumed in *The Wealth of Nations* (1776) that the relationship between buyer and seller is a rational one because the buyer has the intelligence to discriminate between truth and falsity. However, Smith did not anticipate fast-moving images or depth psychology found in modern persuasion. He did not see the day when, in order to keep the economic wheels turning, image technologies would be employed to *create* needs. Advertising is not only concerned with selling products, its power resides in justifying consumption as a way of life. In this way, advertising and corporate-produced electronic images provide an aesthetic, which forms new cultural values. No longer do people judge each other based on moral character, thrift, or productivity. Rather, the criteria for assessing well being are based upon the projection of the self through consumption. While an expressive culture like ours might claim to be egalitarian, it actually favors the most successful expresser, which explains why Hollywood actors, professional athletes, and the famous are held out to us as models and why they receive extremely high salaries. The rest of us sniff for tidbits on the ground. Jardine believes present-day capitalism beares a closer resemblance to Nietzchean morality where God is dead, art is sacred, and self-expression is the common good. Democrats and Republicans both rush to defend consumer capitalism—they only disagree to what extent government or big business should be pulling the levers.

For citizens to be transformed into consumers is a high tragedy after the Huxleyian order. Benjamin R. Barber claims that for consumer capitalism to maintain itself it must create an ethos of infantilization to keep people buying products they don't really need. To feed the consumption machine, children are psychologically manipulated into early adulthood while adults are conditioned to remain in a perpetual state of adolescence. Barber says in *Consumed: How Markets Corrupt Children, Infantilize Adults, and Swallow Citizens Whole*:

> Marketers and merchandisers are self-consciously chasing a youthful commercial constituency sufficiently padded in its pocketbook to be a very attractive market, yet sufficiently unformed in its tastes as to be vulnerable to conscious corporate manipulation via advertising, marketing, and branding. At the same time, these avatars of consumer capitalism are seeking to encourage adult regression, hoping to rekindle in grown-ups the tastes and habits of children so that they can sell globally the relatively useless cornucopia of games, gadgets, and myriad consumer goods for which there is no discernable "need market" other than the one created by capitalism's own frantic imperative to sell.[13]

If this were a matter of peter-panism—adults never wanting to grow up—we might be able to endure it, but global consumer capitalism is not sustainable and will eventually implode upon itself and may be doing so now. Critics of the global economy point out that there are many hidden costs associated with an economic system that has no limits.[14] First, it is expensive to keep producing stuff we don't need and then transporting it across the globe day after day. The practice ravishes ecosystems and depletes natural resources. In a consumer economy, products actually spend most of their existence in a landfill.[15] Second, when corporations produce more and more stuff—and at the same time pay people less and less money—consumers find themselves unable to afford the goods they are producing.

13. Barber, *Consumed*, 7.
14. E.g., see Ransom, "Globalization on the Rocks."
15. See Leonard, "Story of Stuff."

Overproduction leads to layoffs and reduced wages—a dance we are all too familiar with. Third, shifting production overseas creates huge trade imbalances, which leads to more borrowing. The whole system is one that encourages borrowing on both a national and personal level. How can we blame Washington for the national debt crisis when almost every household has a domestic debt crisis of its own? Finally, when adults are kept in a state of perpetual adolescence they cannot be the type of participatory citizens the Founders envisioned. Citizens were supposed to be the stewards of democracy, but instead they are pawns in an incomprehensible game of chess. The great irony of our times is how the free-market has turned out to be not so free; how in the land of choice we have so few choices.

What is called for, in my opinion, is an economic *third way* that would not only meet our material needs but at the same time preserve the identity-forming institutions of family, church, and community. Kirkpatrick Sale says this third way is a society based on "small self-sufficient regions, empowered communities, vibrant neighborhoods, gainfully employed families, individual self satisfactions, decentralized politics, local economies, sustained organic agriculture, cooperative work, environmental humility, and careful nurturing of the earth."[16] For the purposes of this essay we might surmise a third way under three simple precepts: small is beautiful, household economy, and a sacramental ethos that says nature and nature's God should be respected.

Small Is Beautiful

Small can be a hard sell in a world where Big Macs, megachurches, and multinational conglomerates rule the day, but the love of big lends itself to more centralization and less economic freedom. We should move toward de-massification, not massification. There is already a small but growing movement afoot seeking to create local living economies where employees can earn a living wage while producing high-quality products in the context of a locally-based steady market of fair exchange.

For example, Emilia-Romagna is a northern region of Italy consisting of 4.2 million people. Forty-five percent of its GDP comes from eight thousand cooperatively owned enterprises.[17] A cooperative is a business venture

16. Sale, Foreword to *Beyond Capitalism*, xi.

17. See Médaille, *Toward a Truly Free Market*, 227–28, for an Italian version of cooperatives at work.

jointly owned and operated by the people who work there or benefit from its services. Most of these cooperatives are small or medium-sized, and are found in every economic sector from manufacturing, agriculture, finance, retailing, to social services. Not only do these cooperatives work well, but the region's average wage is double that of the average Italian worker.

Small can be both beautiful and profitable. Writer-farmer Wendell Berry has observed that while a typical factory farm might make a huge investment and go into debt to realize a profit of twenty or thirty thousand dollars on the sale of 1.2 million chickens, he knows of a small family-owned-and run farm that can produce two-thousand high quality pastured chickens for a profit of six thousand dollars with little investment for housing or equipment, no large debt, no contract, and no environmental destruction.[18] With regard to larger enterprises Berry says manufacturing should be suited to local needs, locally owned, employ local people, and be non-threatening to the local landscape. He insists "the shop or factory owner should not be an outsider, but rather a sharer in the fate of the place and its community."[19]

Since monopolistic powers tend to squelch free markets and corrupt political systems, there needs to be a return to subsidiary, the belief that higher-level organizations can only justify their existence by the necessary support it gives to lower-level ones. The greatest value should be placed on things closest to us—family, church, and community. Things more distant—state, nation, and world—deserve our allegiance, but only to the degree they can give credence to closer entities. Our problem is that we have reversed this organizing principle so that distant entities have an unjustified control over our lives.

One major factor preventing us from achieving subsidiary is the way electronic media bring what is physically distant into our living rooms. Henry David Thoreau recognized this phenomenon early on with the invention of the telegraph. In 1854 he wrote in *Walden*, "We are in a great haste to construct a magnetic telegraph from Maine to Texas . . . but Maine and Texas, it may be, have nothing to communicate."[20] Communication theorist Neil Postman adds to Thoreau's observation by remarking, "For the first time we were sent information which answered no question we had asked, and

18. See Berry, "Stupidity in Concentration," 18.

19. Berry, "Whole Horse," 113.

20. Quoted in Postman, *Amusing Ourselves to Death*, 65.

which, in any case, did not permit the right of reply."[21] For any third way to be successful, the magic spell of electronic media must be broken so that we are not led around by the nose by distant Conditioners who seek to exploit us for their own profit. Understanding the power advertising and corporate propaganda have over us is a step in the right direction, an exorcism best performed by homes as well as thoughtful schools and churches. Another step toward breaking the spell is to simply avoid pushing the "on" button, something obtained through that old and forgotten virtue called self-control.

Household Economy

Household enterprise was the primary economic unit for thousands of years. Before the seventeenth century, people were identified with their families, not as individuals. No social force yet existed that could dissolve this glue—that is, until industrialization and the subsequent creation of mass society separated the worker from his abode. One might object at this point and say things were different back then, which would be true. But half of all marriages in America now end in divorce, and half of all first marriages are preceded by cohabitation.[22] Nearly 40 percent of all babies in this county are born out of wedlock.[23] Unmarried mothers are three times more likely to suffer from depression,[24] and children of single parent families account for upwards to 80 percent of patients in mental-health institutions.[25] If these statistics are not bad enough, consider that one out of every one hundred Americans is behind bars.[26]

For pre-industrial families the old adage was true: "Families that play together stay together." Likewise, families that worked together stayed together. This is not to say life was trouble-free before the seventeenth century. Pre-industrial life could be extremely harsh. Nevertheless, it must be

---

21. Ibid., 69.

22. Statistics on cohabitation come from Popenoe and Whitehead, "Should We Live Together?," para. 10.

23. Ventura, "Changing Patterns," 6.

24. Davies et al., "Significant Life Experiences," as quoted in Christensen, "Divided," para. 27.

25. Hong and White-Means, "Do Working Mothers," as quoted in Christensen, "Divided," para. 27; Merskey and Swart, "Family Background," as quoted in Christensen, "Divided," para. 27.

26. Liptak, "1 in 100 U.S. Adults Behind Bars," para. 1.

said that pre-industrial families were stronger and more stable in contrast to modern families. Allan Carlson and Paul Mero say in their book *The Natural Family* that in "the pre-industrial order, husbands and wives had specialized in their labor according to their respective strengths and skills so that their small family enterprises might succeed. This natural complementarity reinforced their need for each other, uniting the sexual and the economic functions and giving real strength to the marriage."[27]

In the past men and women were seen as co-laborers—a metaphor beautifully captured in the Garden of Eden, but today men and women are conceptualized as competitors. Beginning in the twentieth century, there was a concerted effort to get women to become a part of the growing industrial economy. Three major factors brought women into the workforce: a rise in service jobs, a decline in the family wage, and more women going to college.[28] Since physical strength is not a requirement for being a knowledge worker, gender preference is much less a factor in the new global order.

Not too long ago *The Atlantic* magazine ran a feature story entitled, "The End of Men: How Women are Taking Control—of Everything." For the first time in American history, women hold the majority of the nation's jobs.[29] The jobs lost in the recent recession—sometimes labeled a *he*-cession—were mostly occupied by men, and of the fifteen job categories projected to grow in the next decade, only two will be primarily occupied by males.[30] This shift is nothing short of a cultural *emasculation*, and it reflects a corporate bias against traditional roles of fathers and mothers.

A third way would seek to revive the old notion of *oikos* or household so that the home is once again seen as a legitimate economic, educational, and care-providing unit. In ancient Greece the home was considered the cornerstone of society and was directly connected with the success of the *polis* or city-state. In most cases the *oikos* was an agricultural unit, but a family-run business certainly would fit its meaning. The household was a fully functioning economic organism with members performing specific roles. When Aristotle speaks of having one's household in order, he means each individual is working for the benefit of the whole. Happiness is conditioned upon finding one's natural place as a member of the functioning household.

27. Carlson and Mero, *Natural Family*, 42.

28. See Flammang, *Taste for Civilization*, 28.

29. Rosin, "End of Men," 60.

30. Ibid.

The home should once again become a center for production, not just consumption. In addition to the creation of cooperatives mentioned above, family farms, cottage industries, and locally own shops should over time outshine agribusiness, multinational corporations, big box distribution centers. Technologies that are highly efficient, rely on renewable energy, and are human-to-scale, if properly appropriated, will make home-based businesses more feasible. The act of schooling your child at home is one of those quintessential third ways. The accelerated growth of the home school movement over the past quarter century is an encouraging sign that parents are seeking out alternatives to bureaucratized education. As the population grows older, the need to care for them will dramatically increase. The home must become a legitimate care-providing unit for the elderly.

The flourishing of cooperative and independent home enterprises will make us rethink the way we order our living spaces and institutions. It will necessitate innovations in city planning and home architecture. It will change the ways we educate people. No longer should we assume that everyone should go to college. Rather, education will be much more diversified and localized. Home schooling, private schools, apprenticeships, and specialized vocational training will play a vital role in educational reform. Another way to support economies of scale is to revitalize guilds. Historically, guilds were associations of craftsmen for a variety of trades. Craft guilds exist today in many European countries and find form in this country in the fields of entertainment, law, real estate, dentistry, and medicine. Guilds have the potential to extend to other fields with regard to training its members, granting licenses, setting professional standards and prices, ensuring product quality, and enforcing safety standards.[31]

Toward a Sacramental Ethos

Accompanying this third way is a deliberate sacramentalism, which recognizes Jefferson's phrase *the laws of nature and nature's God*. It is entirely possible to honor these words without establishing a national religion or yearning for a theocracy. The Founders, influenced by the Enlightenment as they were, allowed for normative notions of truth and were not disturbed by the thought of deriving positive laws from transcendent laws. When Jefferson says the laws of nature are *self-evident*, he means what Aristotle, Augustine,

31. E.g., see Médaille, *Toward a Truly Free Market*, 218–21, for a discussion of how guilds could help save the health care system.

Aquinas, Luther, and Burke meant by it—that God has revealed himself in the Creation and in our conscience. A sacramental ethos believes in a created order from which truth about reality can be drawn; furthermore, through the course of human history civilizations *have* drawn upon it.

In *The Abolition of Man*, C. S. Lewis says natural law, or what he called the *Tao*, tells us to do good and not ill to others, obey authority, honor your parents, love your children, do not lie, and protect those who cannot protect themselves. The *Tao* tells us we are accountable to a higher being. The validity of these truths cannot be deduced. Those who cannot perceive its rationality would not believe its universality anyway. The *Tao* is found throughout all history and in every culture. We need not be afraid to reintroduce natural law moral formulations into the public arena to counter the assumptions associated with naturalistic materialism, especially in the areas of law, economics, and the social sciences.

A sacramental ethos not only acknowledges the laws of nature and nature's God, but it also gives reverence to nature itself. Several decades ago there was a television commercial with a tall, middle-aged woman standing under a tree tasting the contents of a tub of margarine. She is surrounded by animals from the forest and wears a garland of clover. As the shot zooms in she says something about the creamy sweet flavor of butter. Then an off-camera voice corrects her mistake. What is on her finger and lips is not butter, but margarine. Suddenly the woman assumes a dramatic pose, summons thunder and lightning from the sky, and declares, "It's not nice to fool Mother Nature!"

The commercial subtly communicated to the audience that Mother Nature was a buffoon, a force that keeps us from having fun and enjoying newly invented foods like margarine. The immediate meaning of the message was that margarine tastes as good as butter, maybe even better. But the deeper meaning beneath the sales pitch—one that is rooted in the ethos technological societies—is that Mother Nature *can* be fooled, and in fact *deserves* to be fooled.

However, there is a price to be paid for fooling Mother Nature. We ignore her at our own risk. (Perhaps it would be more fitting to call nature our Sister rather than our Mother, as Chesterton pointed out, recognizing the proper subordination.) Nature is not God, and that is why we are forbidden to worship it, but modern society makes a mistake when it separates itself from the Creation for the purpose of exercising dominion over it. The error is not in the exercising of dominion, but in the *separating*.

Techno-industrialism prescribes that we detach ourselves from nature for the purpose of exploiting it, fooling it, manipulating it, or waging war with it. We wish to take the greatest possible advantage of nature, which is the definition of exploitation, and we do not regard the long-term consequences of our actions. T. S. Eliot warned us in *The Idea of a Christian Society* that "a wrong attitude towards nature implies, somewhere, a wrong attitude towards God, and that the consequence is an inevitable doom."[32]

Moving On

Get that degree. Build your resume. Network. Dress for success. Sell yourself. These are the canons of wisdom for landing a job in our modern technological consumerist society, but ask any college graduate looking for work if these shibboleths hold much meaning as they look out over a vast sea of volatility and uncertainty. Our young people did not sign-up for this. Opportunity has been diminished and the remedies for restoring it—apply a stimulus, let the market have free reign, grow jobs—ring hollow because deep down we know something is terribly wrong with our economic ordering. We must start building something else, something more humane and compatible with the real world and our own limits. Even Dorothy realized the Emerald City was not what she really was looking for, that what she really wanted was to go back home. It's time to go back home. There, we will find something to do.

Oh I've finally decided my future lies beyond the yellow brick road.

---

32. Eliot, *Idea of a Christian Society*, 62.

7

Oikos

A Case for Reviving the Household Economy

Your wife will be like a fruitful vine within your house; Your children will be like olive shoots around your table.[1]

ONE OF THE MORE effective strategies in converting an Anabaptist to a Pedobaptist is to have him examine the ancient term "household." It certainly worked in my case as I poured over literature handed to me by kind elders and teachers who not only wanted me to feel at home in a new denomination but also knew a little nudge might pull me over to the entire creed. I read Jonathan Watt's "The *Oikos* Formula" in *The Case for Covenantal Infant Baptism*, and it soon became apparent that baptism was not so much a sign of my personal faith as it was a sign of the Faithful One on my behalf and on behalf of my family. It put the account of the Philippian jailer, Lydia's household, and other family baptisms in an entirely new light. Once I connected the continuity between New Testament baptism and Old Testament circumcision, the light bulb went off, and voila! A Pedobaptist I became.

Very Different from Our Ancestors

My transition to pedobaptistry was remarkably smooth, but the investigation that brought me to it raised new questions. I could not help but think about the kind of life that existed under *oikos*, where the father was

1. Ps 128:3 ESV.

master, the mother was a kind of domestic executor, and the children were successors in-training. There might have also been extended family in the household, as well as apprentices, hired labor and servants. It nagged on me. To think that for thousands of years the household enterprise was not only a social unit, but an economic one was both baffling and intellectually stimulating. Perhaps I had not paid attention to my sociology professor, or maybe she had not dwelt upon it, but up until the seventeenth century, most work was carried out at home, not away. Men and women, boys and girls, worked together in the same vicinity. Tasks on the farm were determined by tradition, need, and ability best suited to one's sex. The men and boys plowed, hedged, carted, and performed the skilled work associated with the harvest. The women and girls kept house, looked after livestock, went to market, prepared meals, and made butter, cheese, bread, and beer. During harvest everyone was in the field—man and woman, boy and girl. These kinds of arrangements were not only true for the countryside but also the shop. Peter Laslet writes in *The World we have lost*, "Time was when the whole of life went forward in the family, in a circle of loved, familiar faces, known and fondled objects, all to human size. . . . It makes us very different than our ancestors."[2]

My investigation of *oikos* made me wonder if the totality of what we have gained in the last two hundred years or more is preferable to the totality of what we have lost. On one hand we have much to be thankful for—air conditioning, anesthesia, and automobiles. On the other hand we have much to be concerned about—atomic bombs, seductive advertising, and easy annulments. What tugged on my mind was whether personal comfort and higher mobility was a fair trade-off for the erosion of social cohesion.

Far from being an economic unit, the home today functions more as temporary sleeping quarters and entertainment center for self-actualizing individuals. Studies now show that most married couples consider personal happiness more important than having children. Only a third of American households contain children, and less than a fourth of households consist of a father, mother, and children.[3] While personal happiness might justify a couple's coming together, it just as easily justifies their coming apart. The statistic by now is trite because of its redundancy, but it still remains that

2. Laslet, *World We Have Lost*, 21.

3. U.S. Bureau of the Census, "America's Families and Living Arrangements," as quoted in Flammang, *Taste for Civilization*, 44.

half of all American marriages end in divorce, and this is true of evangelical marriages as well.

Even pastors in Reformed churches would perhaps agree that their congregants struggle with the same kinds of difficulties found outside of the church—getting past the pain of a broken home, balancing family and work, stretching a shrinking income check, and managing personal debt. Modern families today have few buttresses of moral support outside the local church, and even then, the support may be minimal. In his book *An Unexpected Journey* Robert Godfrey describes how the loss of community puts more pressure on the church to provide some kind of solace:

> Community is threatened in many ways in our modern world. Most of us do not live in traditional neighborhoods. Oh, we have neighbors, but at most we have only a nodding acquaintance with almost all of them. No real sense of community exists in many apartment buildings, condos, and suburban streets. The result is often a sense of isolation and alienation. Our families too, as communities today, are at risk. So many marriages end in divorce that community is often broken between parents and for children. Even in families that are not broken by divorce, the busyness of life is a grave problem. Whether at work, on the road, at school or at lessons for children outside of school, or even at church, families often have little time together, except perhaps to watch TV.[4]

It's the Economic Stupor

I used to think the demise of the traditional family was due to deep moral decay brought on by secularization. However, I now believe this is only part of the problem. About the same time I was handed *The Case for Covenantal Infant Baptism* another person slipped me a copy of the even more subversive *What Are People For?*, by Wendell Berry. In the essay, "Feminism, the Body, and the Machine," the agrarian author claims we have arrived at a situation in which marriage is no longer viewed as a state of mutual help between two partners.[5] Berry's point is that mutuality becomes a natural and necessary ingredient for a marriage when the home is a place of production and not just consumption. However, modern societies now hold such mutuality in contempt. Berry says, "Men in general

4. See Godfrey, "Experiencing a Congregation, Psalm 84," 29.
5. Berry, "Feminism," 178–96.

were the first to hold it in contempt as they departed from it for the sake of the professional salary or the hourly wage."[6] Women were the second to hold it in contempt as they departed for the same reason. Berry does not wish to take issue with people, men or women, who find it necessary to work outside the home. He merely wants to ask why we should consider this a desirable state of things.

The reason we consider both parents working outside the home as desirable may have less to do with any contempt on our part and more with societal and economic conditioning. Our culture is now fully equipped with a kind of "surround sound" of consumption that instructs us from birth to believe our main purpose in life is to be a perpetual shopper. In his book *Amusing Ourselves to Death* Neil Postman suggests Aldous Huxley's happy-faced totalitarianism was the truer prophecy to George Orwell's sad-faced totalitarianism. The greatest danger for our culture is that we would be ruined by what we loved (pleasure) rather than what we hated (pain): "Huxley feared we would become a trivial culture, preoccupied with some equivalent of the feelies, the orgy porgy, and the centrifugal bumblepuppy."[7] It was Huxley who said in *Brave New World Revisited* that the civil libertarians and rationalists, who are ever on the alert to oppose tyranny, "failed to take into account man's almost infinite appetite for distractions."[8]

Rhetorician and historian Richard Weaver argues in his classic work, *Ideas Have Consequences*, that the most effective promoter of progressive materialism—even more effective than secular education—is the Great Stereopticon, by which he means the new information environment, or what we might dub contemporary media. In 1948, when his book was published, this included the press, the motion picture industry, and radio (television had not fully taken off). Weaver says the combined function of this "machine" is to "project selected pictures of life in the hope that what is seen will be imitated."[9] Weaver's claim is that media are the technological means by which stereotypes are multiplied so that we are constantly assured the goal in life is personal happiness through the maintenance of comfort. The voices and the faces that occupy the media tell us everything is going to be fine. The announcer is cheery and optimistic even when the news is bad. Today we might say the commercial that follows the news story—even a horrific

---

6. Ibid., 181.

7. Postman, *Amusing Ourselves to Death*, vii.

8. Quoted from ibid., viii.

9. Weaver, *Ideas Have Consequences*, 93.

news story—still tells us to keep buying. Weaver says the proprietors of the Stereopticon know what they want and what they are doing: "They are protecting a materialistic civilization growing more insecure and panicky as awareness filters through that it is over an abyss."[10] Although the Great Stereopticon seems to make us informed citizens, it actually insulates us from wisdom by frustrating our contemplation of the flow of history. The lack of reflection on the past it imposes—the recoiling of memory—keeps us in a kind of hypnotic trance and we cannot remember our former selves.

We can no longer remember when life was connected to the home or when communities were living things. An initial exposure to someone like Berry or Weaver might produce a reaction of denial; a response that acknowledges the benefits of strong families and communities but denies economics had anything to do with their demise. There are two obstacles that prevent us from seeing what Berry and Weaver are saying. First, we equate our current economic system with virtue and freedom. Second, we believe the only alternative to our current economic system is socialism or communism. However, both of these assumptions are flawed.

Consumerism, Capitalism, and Distributism

We rarely entertain the thought that our current economic system might actually produce less virtuous people and at the same time retard real freedom. The Alliance of Confessing Evangelicals has eloquently and faithfully decried the crass consumerist mentality that has wreaked havoc on the evangelical church, but what of its overall effect on the culture? What is bad for the goose is also bad for the gander. Consumerism is a materialistic philosophy whereby the common good is reduced to the acquisition of goods and services. Furthermore, it is predicated on unlimited growth—an "expand or die" proposition that will not stop until every resource is sucked out of the earth to the detriment of future generations. If everyone became the type of consumer that exists in America we would need seven times more of the world's finite resources than actually are known to exist to sustain ourselves.[11] The virtues of love, joy, peace, patience, kindness, generosity, gentleness, and self-control have little to do with the maintenance of consumerism, yet these virtues have everything to do with healthy families and communities.

10. Ibid., 106.

11. See Dernbach, "In Focus," as quoted in Pearce, *Small Is Still Beautiful*, 57–58.

Consumerism is, of course, connected to many of our notions about capitalism, and to some people criticizing any aspect of capitalism is akin to questioning the miracles of the Apostles. Many Christians somehow think Moses at Mount Sinai established capitalism, when, in fact, it did not become a dominant economic system in the West until the nineteenth century. In truth, modern capitalism often manifests itself in the concentration of wealth in powerful monopolies, which ironically has the tendency to squelch free enterprise. This is why family farms and independent shops do not flourish in modern capitalist societies. And this is why G. K. Chesterton quipped, "Too much capitalism does not mean too many capitalists, but too few capitalists."

Chesterton and his contemporary Hilaire Belloc argued that modern capitalism was an unstable force and in conflict with moral theories of liberty. One has only to read a Charles Dickens novel to get a picture of unbridled capitalism. By the beginning of the twentieth century it was recognized that monopolistic capitalism had to be undergirded by government-initiated programs and entitlements to ensure its stability. Thus, big business and big government work in tandem to form what Belloc called the "Servile State," whereby an unfree majority of non-owners work for the pleasure of a free minority of owners.

Chesterton and Belloc supported a "third way" economic system called distributism, which should not be confused with socialism or communism, systems which also concentrate wealth and power in the hands of a few. Distributism is an economic philosophy, which sees the widest use of private productive property as the most desirable economic system to ensure true liberty and prosperity. An American version of distributism is perceived in Thomas Jefferson's vision of an agrarian society. A Russian version of distributism is reflected in Alexander Solzhenitsyn's "democracy of small places." Adopting a third way economic arrangement does not mean going back to the bleakness of the Middle Ages or that we all again must take up plows. Distribution has more to do with creating a human living environment that is economically decentralized, aesthetically pleasing, and technologically deliberate. Distributism is essentially a humane microcapitalism, a reverting back to community and regional-centered economies. Third way advocates place the family at the heart of society rather than the individual. Rod Dreher says in his book *Crunchy Cons* that small, local, and old are to be preferred over big, global, and new. "We affirm the superiority of the free market as an economic organizing principle," explains Dreher, "but believe the economy must be made to serve humanity's best interests, not the other way around."[12]

12. See Dreher, "Crunchy Con Manifesto," 1–2.

The Weber Thesis Revisited

The topic of household economy would not be complete without some discussion of the so-called "Weber Thesis." The sociologist Max Weber was careful to define what he meant by capitalism, something he says had always existed, but in these latter days had become the dominant economic order in the West. Capitalism, he says, is the pursuit of profit by the systematic means of continuous and rational enterprise.[13] Weber believed the organization of a free labor force is what distinguished the old capitalism from the new, and he says modern capitalism would not be possible without two factors: the separation of business from the household and rational book-keeping which kept a focused eye on the bottom line. The Weber Thesis asserts that in order for capitalism to take hold as a dominant economic force it had to get past religious sentiment, which in the past had frowned upon systematic wealth accumulation. Elements within Protestantism, specifically the Calvinistic view of vocational calling, provided the religious and psychological sanctions needed to justify rational productive labor.

Weber's method of inquiry, which has been criticized as unscientific, does not permit him to establish a direct cause-effect relationship between Protestantism and capitalism, but neither did he claim as much. Certainly there were other important factors that summoned the spirit of capitalism besides Calvin's view of work. For example, Weber does not mention the role of the printing press as a prototype of mass production. Also, the capitalistic spirit was already present in Venice and Florence in the fourteenth century and in Antwerp in the fifteenth century.[14] Neither does Weber imply that the early Reformers were capitalists themselves. To the contrary, neither Luther nor Calvin endorsed the worldly pursuit of wealth. What Weber is addressing is the ethos of Protestantism and how a particular interpretation of calling helped legitimize free labor just prior to the major democratic movements in North America and Europe.

Luther's teaching on vocation was distinctive because it held that all work, not just the work of the clergy, could be a sacred calling. Calvinism also embraced this view, but had followers who placed a heavier emphasis on the notion that everyone must labor in their calling. This was a subtle difference, but an important one. Whereas Luther's contribution to vocational calling emphasized the role of providence through birth and station,

13. Weber, *Protestant Ethic and the Spirit of Capitalism*, 17.
14. See "Translator's Preface," in Ibid., 7.

Calvinism came to emphasize productive work and the sin of idleness. Weber says Luther's perspective possessed limited transformational potency because it essentially remained a traditionalist view of calling. One could be born into a poor station in life and remain there and still be found in God's sovereign will. But Paul's admonition that he "who will not work shall not eat" told the Calvinist that idleness was a symptom of a lack of grace.

Weber points out that in the medieval world Paul's words about work carried a softer edge. Aquinas interpreted Paul's admonition as the natural way the individual and the community maintained themselves; it was a principle rather than a strict command.[15] In America we are still living off the borrowed capital of our Protestant work ethic. Consequently, it dominates the current utilitarian thrust of modern economics. Pulitzer Prize winner Marilynne Robinson, a Calvinist, puts her finger on the new ethos when she shrewdly comments, "Lately we have been told and told again that our educators are not preparing American youth to be efficient workers. Workers. That language is so common among us now that an extraterrestrial might think we had actually *lost* the Cold War."[16]

This is not to say the regimented life could not be found in the medieval world, even as a spiritual duty, for it existed inside the monastery. Catholicism kept the alert rational life at bay through the ascetic life of the monk. However, under the Protestant view of vocation the emphasis on activity would, in the end, minimize the notion of *place*. For Puritans like Richard Baxter it did not matter if labor was connected to the home or found in the factory, as long as the individual remained busy and productive. Weber notes how Baxter more than once expressed what would become Adam Smith's apotheosis of the division of labor, that specialization of occupation can improve production, thus serving the common good, which was not far removed from the good of the greatest possible number. Weber points out that Baxter's utilitarian outlook was consistent with the secular literature at that time promoting capitalism.[17]

Weber levies the familiar arguments against Calvin's doctrine of predestination, which he claims was the most important element within the political and cultural struggles of the sixteenth and seventeenth centuries. He considers the doctrine extremely inhumane and suggests that it must have had the effect of producing feelings of unprecedented inner loneliness for

15. See ibid., 159.
16. Robinson, *When I Was a Child I Read Books*, 24.
17. Weber, *Protestant Ethic and the Spirit of Capitalism*, 161.

the individual.[18] He somehow assumes that Calvinists spent much of their time in a state of despair, unsure from one day to the other if they were one of God's elect. A more careful analysis of Calvin's teachings would show that the Reformer held a certain antinomy towards human will and divine sovereignty, that predestination was more of an unresolved puzzle rather than a simple determinism or fatalism. Weber's understanding of Calvinistic soteriology would insist that assurance of salvation came only through objective evidence of good works. He overlooks, however, the more subjective and personal assurances taught by Calvin such as heart-felt faith in a benevolent God and genuine love for the church. His skewed view of the doctrine of predestination forces him to conclude that Calvinists were destined to end up on the same plane with Franklin, namely, that God helps those who help themselves. Weber overstates his case when he asserts that productive work was for the Puritan the "most evident" proof of his salvation.[19]

Weber's misjudgment of the doctrine of predestination and its foreboding effects he thought it had on the Puritan mind does not diminish the credibility of his overall thesis—that the Calvinistic view of calling came to play a major role in the ethical justification of free labor. The Weber Thesis, like Calvinism itself, easily reduces to caricature so that if exposed to a brief version of it one might be left thinking the Reformers preached wealth acquisition from their pulpits or would have rejoiced had they seen the consumerism of our own day. Weber candidly admits this was not the case; it was a second generation of Calvinists that were compelled to place their blessing on specialized labor, and it was not until after the religious fervor of Puritanism died out that utilitarian worldliness set in making it permissible for the contemporary capitalist to assert, "Greed is good."

Keep in mind this little analysis of Weber is coming from a Calvinist, be it one who finds significant value in Roman Catholic social theory, which by-the-way, more Calvinists should pay attention to, if not embrace altogether as their own, especially the principles of familialism, subsidiarity, and solidarity. Capitalism probably would have gotten off the ground even without a nod from the Protestant clergy, so we need not raise our pointed fingers too quickly in the direction of Calvin. The Enlightenment favored innovation and change as much as the Reformation, if not more. Might it also be said that the First Great Awakening, and to a larger degree the Second Great Awakening, convulsed parish and communal life

18. See ibid., 104.

19. See ibid., 172.

and were themselves conducted in spirit of progress influenced heavily by the Enlightenment and industrialism?[20] Certainly capitalism favored—was made for in fact—hard working Protestants who loved their families, built communities, and practiced the virtue of self-control, but from America's inception there was this killer gene that would always make wealth accumulation the default value when spiritual and aesthetic values waned. Carl Trueman, Professor of Historical Theology and Church History at Westminster Theological Seminary, summed-up the trajectory of capitalism like this: "If Weber was right, then the best we can say is (to put it in really broad strokes): (a) Protestantism turbo-charged capitalism; (b) capitalism fuelled consumerism; and (c) consumerism found unnecessary—if not downright inconvenient as hindrances to growth—the values which fuelled (a) and thus slowly but surely eroded them to nothing."[21]

Homeboys and Homegirls

If the household economy were to be revitalized, it would mean that men, women, and children would spend more time at home. To the modern mind, the admonition that women should be "keepers at home"[22] is both oppressive and demeaning—oppressive because it relegates women to an older sphere from which they have been liberated; demeaning because modern "housework," it is sometimes said, requires minimal intelligence. Historian Ruth Schwartz Cowan points out in *More Work for Mother*, that the term *housework* would be nonsensical to a pre-modern because before the Industrial Revolution *all* work was done around the home.[23] The terms *housewife* and *husband* entered the English language around the thirteenth century and referred to work that took place on one's residence. The word husband is derived from *hus*, which means *house*, and *band*, which means *bonded*. Both husband and wife were bound to the land. The husband was tied to it because he held the title. The wife was tied to it through marriage to her husband. Likewise, the term *husbandry* refers to someone who worked the land that surrounded the home.

Before industrialization the husband and children shared in the household tasks, especially work that brought food to the table. As we have already

20. Hart makes this point in "Wendell Berry's Unlikely Case," 141–44.

21. Trueman, "Weber Again," n.p.

22. Titus 2:5 ESV.

23. See Cowan, *More Work for Mother*.

pointed out, this work was reciprocal: "women assisted men in the fields, and men helped women with household foodwork. Husbands and children helped housewives with cooking and baking by chopping wood, shelling corn, pounding grain into meal, collecting coal, and making sausages,"[24] but with the introduction of new technologies in the nineteenth century, such as the cast-iron cooking stove, the automatic flour mill, and factory-produced food and clothing, the labor of the husband and children became less needed. The husband found wage labor work in town, and the chores of the children diminished over time. The work of women around the home actually increased during the nineteenth century even though families were buying more laborsaving devices. By the middle of the twentieth century, women were being allured away from the home as the men had been centuries earlier. Although they now had wage labor jobs, women were still expected to do the "housework" when they came home. Despite all the sirens telling her to be liberated from the home, there was more work for mother than before. Fortunately, when the TV dinner, microwave oven, and the fast food restaurant came along, her burden was somewhat lifted, even if the taste of the food and the fellowship around the table was compromised.

Women who were liberated from their homes became subservient to new bosses. Although Chesterton's remark predates the exodus that occurred a generation after his time, it captured one of the great ironies associated with women moving into the workforce: "Ten thousand women marched through the streets of London saying we will not be dictated to, and then went off to become stenographers."[25] Our radical egalitarianism makes us run from the word "submission," even though it is still to be found at all levels of society from government, to the corporate world, to the church. Hierarchy is built into the created order, and we need not deny its functionality or its presence, especially in the home. The biblical teaching, which is grounded in the created order, is that it is good and right for wives to follow their husband's leadership. Submission ideally takes place in the context of a true partnership, in which the husband values his wife's companionship and counsel and the wife values her husband's leadership.[26]

The virtuous woman in Proverbs 31 is an *oikos* woman, and her work is hardly oppressive or demeaning. The heart of her husband trusts in her because without her heroic contribution, the household will come to ruin.

24. Flammang, *Taste for Civilization*, 27.

25. See Ffinch, *G. K. Chesterton*, 180.

26. Köstenberger, *God, Marriage, and Family*, 73.

She seeks wool and flax, and works with willing hands. She rises while it is night and provides food for her household and portions for her maidens. She considers a field and buys it. She plants a vineyard. She opens her hand to the poor. She makes linen garments and sells them. She delivers sashes to the merchant. Wisdom and kindness are on her tongue. She looks well to the ways of her *household*. She does not eat the bread of idleness. Her children rise up and call her blessed. Her husband praises her. This is a workingwoman, but her devotion and loyalty reside in what is closest to her—spouse, offspring, and dwelling place. There is an undeniable beauty to such affection if one is not blinded by the false notion that bosses, office spouses, and daycare workers are preferable to fathers and mothers. I am not saying women should be found at home as a categorical imperative any more than I am saying men should be found at home as a categorical imperative. What our attention should be drawn to with regard to the issue of women working outside the home are the needs of the children and the great potential of diversity that can be found in managing a household.

More illumination on the household woman can be found in Paul's instruction to Timothy on the subject of widows. After Paul gives the qualifications of a widow worthy of honor and sets her age limit, he then counsels the younger widows to marry, bear children, and manage their households. By doing this, they will not give the adversary (Satan) an occasion for slander.[27] Paul is holding out an ideal for the Christian woman, an ideal that has its fullest texture within the context of a household economy where members of the family are producers, not just consumers. Likewise, when the Psalmist says, "Your wife will be like a fruitful vine within your house; your children will be like olive shoots around your table,"[28] the agricultural metaphor is not lost on the common Hebrew who cultivated a garden next to the house. The metaphor offers a picture of the organic nature of the household, one where work, education, and play existed together in one place.

It is interesting how the *Shema Yisrael*—considered the most important passage of the Torah—is connected to the household:

> Hear, O Israel: The LORD our God, the LORD is one. You shall love the LORD your God with all your heart and with all your soul and with all your might. And these words that I command you today shall be on your heart. You shall teach them diligently to your children, and shall talk of them when you sit in your house, and when

27. 1 Tim 5:14 ESV.
28. Ps 128:3 ESV.

you walk by the way, and when you lie down, and when you rise. You shall bind them as a sign on your hand, and they shall be as frontlets between your eyes. You shall write them on the doorposts of your house and on your gates.[29]

Raising a family is a daunting task when an aggressive and ubiquitous culture has more influence over the children than the parents. Children are seemingly unprotected against corporate interests seeking to lure little Johnny into becoming an active consumer before he utters his first words. What effect chemical compounds are having on his growing body we are not certain. He is not yet a teenager, and yet he runs the risk of being obese. We are not sure what the intended or unintended curriculums are teaching him at school. He spends more time with electronic media than he does in the presence of teachers or parents. Violent and sexual images are a click away. He sits there absorbed in the screen, and as much as we try, we cannot pull him away. Someone or something has kidnapped him. No wonder John Bakan, a law professor at the University of British Columbia, writes in a *New York Times* op-ed, "There is reason to believe that childhood itself is now in crisis."[30]

If the home is little more than a temporary sleeping quarters and entertainment center, then yes, housework requires little intelligence, and might even be considered demeaning. But what if the home was a place of production? What if it was a place where children received their initial education? What if it was a place where elderly parents lived out their twilight years? What kind of intelligence would be required to manage *that* kind of household? Again, Chesterton reminds us that by partly limiting and protecting women from the work-a-day world outside the home, she was able to have five or six professions and play at a hundred trades. He says, "This is what has been really aimed at from the first in what is called the seclusion, or even the oppression, of women. Women were not kept at home in order to keep them narrow; on the contrary, they were kept at home in order to keep them broad."[31]

Not only would a revival of the household economy require broad women, it would also require broad men. Instead of trying to escape the material reality of a tangible world, embracing the obscure forces of a global marketplace, we should be bringing things closer to home where we

29. Deut 11:13–17 ESV.

30. Bakan, "Kids Are Not All Right," para. 2.

31. Chesterton, "Emancipation of Domesticity," 128.

can put our hands on them. Matthew Crawford says in this excellent book, *Shop Class as Soulcraft* that we need to once again "feel that our world is intelligible, so we can be responsible for it."[32] The current economic crisis should make us reconsider our assumptions about an arrangement where no one seems to be able to nail anything down. Crawford says, "The question of what a good job looks like—of what sort of work is both secure and worthy of being honored—is more open now than it has been for a long time."[33] He calls for the revitalization of manual trades, craftsmanship, and self-reliance. Crawford believes the love of vocation can once again be found in working with both our minds and hands together.

Not everyone can or wants to be a farmer or a shop owner, but microcapitalism is predicated on more people being their own boss, even if that means the business is jointly owned and operated by a group of people who have formed a co-op. Jefferson believed that having many productive property owners made democracy more secure because it produced citizens who had a compelling interest to participate. Instead of having a society where wealth and power are concentrated in the hands a few—which only leads to exploitation and alienation—the need of the hour is to encourage more self-reliant enterprises to flourish. This keeps state and corporate power in check and at the same time strengthens families and local communities.

This is all fairly simple to understand; it is much more difficult to implement. The powers that be are interested in keeping their power, and it will be no easy task to compel them to let go of it. But if we must have an economic system that requires both spouses to work then we should at least try to keep families and communities together and let the profits go to them. As Allan C. Carlson explains, initiating incentives toward decentralization and safe guarding smaller economic entities, the family being primary, does this.[34] According to Carlson the nuts and bolts of a governmental policy that would favor the natural family would include reintroducing "fault" into divorce laws, viewing marriage as a full economic partnership, expanding income tax exemptions and tax credits for families with children, recognizing the societal benefit of large families, protecting home education, deconsolidating public schools to single-school districts, loosening laws that restrict home businesses and home schools, ending centralizing regulations toward professions like law and medicine so that

32. Crawford, *Shop Class as Soulcraft*, 8.
33. Ibid., 9.
34. See Carlson and Mero, "Natural Family Policy."

they would benefit from other arrangements such as apprenticeships, re-structuring Medicare and Social Security through tax credits that favors childbearing and family-centered elder care, and strengthening parental rights toward children.[35]

Transform the Culture into What?

I do not place my case for reviving the household economy under the auspices of the Great Commission because I do not think it is the responsibility of the church to intentionally affect societal change on economic or political grounds. *Intentionally*, it is not in the church's purview; *unintentionally*, the church obviously affects change in society. The revitalization of *oikos* should have the effect of strengthening the family unit, which in turn would strengthen our churches.

D. A. Carson makes a distinction between the responsibilities of the "church" and the responsibilities of "Christians" in his book, *Christ & Culture Revisited*.[36] The church is where the gospel is faithfully proclaimed, where the sacraments are rightly observed, and where godly corporate discipline operates. Christians, while benefactors of the gospel ministry, serve God in their various vocations as salt in a corrupt world, as light, and as in Jeremiah's day, doing good in the place where they live.[37] Reviving the household economy is a worthwhile pursuit under the cultural mandate, that is, mankind's obligation to be fruitful and multiply, and to exercise dominion over the earth.[38]

I quickly learned in Reformed circles that Christians are supposed to be transforming the culture for Christ. But I soon came to question the *telos* of the proposition. Transform the culture into what? What would the culture look like if Christians were to transform it? Carson is correct in saying there is some truth to be found in each of Richard Niebuhr's categories respective to a Christian's relationship to culture, from separating from it, to synthesizing it, to straddling it, and transforming it. If there is any merit to a transformational

---

35. Carlson and Mero define the natural family "to be the union of a man and a woman through marriage for the purposes of sharing love and joy, propagating children, providing their moral education, building a vital home economy, offering security in times of trouble, and binding the generations," in ibid., 13.

36. See Carson, *Christ & Culture Revisited*, 151–52.

37. Jer 29:1–7 ESV.

38. Gen 1:26–30 ESV.

aspect of the cultural mandate, then what better task can we set for ourselves than to strengthen our homes, churches, and local communities? (Again, this question is not meant to devalue the supreme value of declaring the gospel. And certainly the gospel has transformation import in itself.)

I would not want to suggest there is a particular society or economic system better suited for Christianity. The church has thrived in all sorts of societies and under all sorts of economic conditions. I would rather suggest there is a kind of society and a kind of economic system, from a historical perspective, that is more at harmony with the moral theories of liberty, more reflective of the created order, and better suited for the family. Nothing about our participatory democracy should prevent us from working ourselves out of a dysfunctional ordering and moving toward a better one; nay, our system demands it.

Although clear distinctions exist between the Great Commission and the cultural mandate, this does not mean the two realms should never meet. They do in fact meet when a local church establishes a Christian school. An attempt to establish parish life around deliberate neighborhoods is a possible area where both gospel and cultural mandates might be brought together—but cautiously.

Andy Crouch has argued that Christians should not just be in the business of condemning culture, and neither should we be copying culture. Instead, we should be creating culture.[39] In Shakespeare's *Henry V* the king of England, after subduing France, gently whispers in the ear of his princess bride: "Dear Kate, you and I cannot be confined within the weak list of a country's fashion: we are the makers of manners . . ."

Reviving the household economy is a creative act whereby we make anew.

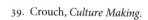

39. Crouch, *Culture Making*.

8

Back to the Shire

From English Village to Global Village, and Back Again

At last the hobbits had their faces turned towards home.[1]

ANOTHER WAVE OF MIDDLE-EARTH lore has come our way as Hollywood offers up three installments of *The Hobbit*, J. R. R. Tolkien's prequel to *The Lord of the Rings*. As with the *Ring* trilogy, the story of *The Hobbit* is anchored in the Shire, a place where "peace and quiet and good tilled earth" are held out as ideals of the good life.

We are attracted to the Shire for the same reasons we are drawn to those little window-lit figurine buildings, resting on a bed of cotton snow, displayed in Walmart during the Christmas season. The Kinkadesque homes, churches, and mercantile stores remind us of a time lost, a time when, perhaps, people were happier and rooted to something more permanent. Few of us make the connection between the big box store we are standing in and the disappearance of what the display in Walmart signifies. But in truth one smashed the other. The big global village ate the little local village.

Shire Living

Strictly speaking, a shire is any county belonging to Great Britain. However, if we define it as Tolkien idealized it, then the Shire is a community of people

---

1. Tolkien, *Return of the King*, 967.

dependent upon each other and to the land that contains it, striving to live in a continual state of harmony and peace according to nature and nature's God.

Loss-of-community grievers like me sometimes wonder if it is possible to lay claim again to the Shire. The subject is difficult because what all progressives loath—and we are all progressives now—is any suggestion that we ought to "go back" to something older, slower, and simpler. Visions of toil, premature death, and loss of hard-won freedoms dance in the head so that the conversation never gets beyond, "What do you mean more of us should grow our own food?"

I am not Amish, but Presbyterian, and I am not suggesting we return to the days of slavery, travel by horseback, or surgery without anesthesia. I am just wondering if there is a place within the American Dream where agrarians and New Urbanists can carve out an alternative way of living that is not as artificial and volatile as what we have now, and what continues to swell up and engulf our lives.

Despite all its obvious shortcomings, at least pre-industrial society possessed a certain *ecology of life* where family, church, and community were interwoven. But these old identity-forming institutions have been dismantled under the shadow of technological society, a low-humming Machine that recognizes no common good but the values of a marketplace gone hyper-consumer.

I am compelled to agree with the French social theorist Jacques Ellul who said that "we have forgotten our collective ends . . . . In this terrible dance of means which have been unleashed, no one knows where we are going, the aim of life has been forgotten, the end has been left behind. Man has set out a tremendous speed—to go *nowhere*."[2]

Shire living existed for thousands of years and is not exclusively Christian. Thomas Jefferson idealized it, as did Cicero. Christianity, however, brings unique elements to it. Tolkien's Shire is a Christian culture to be sure, although vaguely so because his story is non-allegorical. Nevertheless, he sheaths his Christian metaphysics in a world similar to our own.

Middle-earth is the world before the assembly line, electricity, modern advertising, and social planning. So we might say Tolkien's habitation of hobbits is based on a pre-industrial English village. He even claimed as much, saying that Bag End was patterned after the Worchester countryside.[3]

---

2. Ellul, *Presence of the Kingdom*, 63, 69.

3. See Carpenter, *Tolkien*, 176.

In the early seventeenth century, three-fourths of England lived in or close to a country village. A typical Elizabethan community was composed of about seventy families, each averaging four or five members.[4] These were close-knit social units, bound by common beliefs and behavior.

Despite any disagreements the Puritans had with the Church of England, they still considered themselves English and therefore carried over with them the laws and customs of the mother country. Early colonial towns were actually transplants of medieval-like villages with the primary difference being that the settlers were not tenants, but land owners who had pledged themselves to a covenanted corporation.

Once the Massachusetts Bay Company was up and running, entire congregations made the voyage across the Atlantic to form townships, each averaging about thirty-five square miles. Most New England towns consisted of a central church building, a town hall, a school, and a village green. Radiating from the hub were the homes, and farther out the farms and common pasture lands. These towns observed agreed-upon limits and stopped granting lots once an optimum size was reached.

The citizens of the Puritan communal system made a conscious attempt to build the most perfect society they could possibly arrange for themselves. They possessed a postmillennial eschatology that gave them reason to be optimistic about their community-building endeavors; they were, after all, going to help usher in the Kingdom of God. We who are accustomed to pluralism wonder why the Puritans could not have developed some kind of theory of toleration. What we fail to understand is that *all* peasant utopias, the medieval norm, were closed societies, whether Catholic or Calvinist.[5]

By the time Jonathan Edwards had established himself in Northampton, Massachusetts, four generations removed from the landing of the *Mayflower*, the capitalist market revolution was making itself known in the American hinterlands. Edwards did not care for how the new freewheeling economics based on self-regulation was affecting his congregants. He noted how individual interests and personal ambition rather than the common good increasingly motivated community members. Liberal capitalism had the potential to bring out the worst in human nature; therefore, he

4. Bremer, *Puritan Experiment*, 172.

5. See Lockridge, *New England Town*, 19.

preferred price regulation by magistrates.[6] He saw the new economic order, as he did almost everything, as a moral issue.

On the Road to Mordor

By mid-eighteenth century, the Puritan experiment of community building had come to an end. After a century, many original townships had reached their population limits. The young and restless were compelled to move on to unsettled areas.[7] The Great Awakening undercut the authority of the pastors and elders who had been the stewards of wisdom and truth. "I won't worship a wig!" complained a Northampton youth brought before a church discipline committee.[8] He was referring to what was on Edward's head. The little episode foreshadowed the removal of the minister as a primary arbitrator of truth in Western society. The Awakening enlarged the notion of religious liberty and eventually infused itself with New England politics where a younger generation, the New Lights, saw individual freedom as a desirable quality for a new nation. On the Eve of the Revolution, it could easily be said that the Puritan had become a Yankee.

It is an interesting coincidence of history that the *Wealth of Nations* was published in the same year of the Declaration of Independence. Adam Smith's treatise challenged the old Mercantile System, claiming it was outdated and needed to be replaced with a more "perfect liberty" in which state-sponsored restrictions on trade were removed. America, sitting there, largely unexplored and unexploited, added impetus to Smith's argument. In effect, Smith wanted to shift the economic locus from the nation to the world.

Rational calculation, standardization, and specialization—the accepted tools of science—were now applied to economics as a controlling technique. If the correct technique were applied, a factory could produce 48,000 pins a day through the division of labor. As Ellul points out in *The Technological Society*, the Industrial Revolution would have never occurred were it not for this kind of technical intention.[9] Due to the socio-political

6. See Marsden, *Jonathan Edwards*, 303–4. See also Murray, *Jonathan Edwards*, 85–86, for Edward's view of the changes in Northampton under an increasing free-market economy.

7. This pattern is documented in Bushman, *From Puritan to Yankee*.

8. See Marsden's account of the "young folks' Bible" case in *Jonathan Edwards*, 298–302.

9. See Ellul, *Technological Society*, 43.

upheavals created by the Renaissance, the Reformation, and the swelling Enlightenment, Europe was much more malleable than it had been two centuries earlier. England and France led the way in new methods of agriculture and commerce, which reduced the small landowner and the yeoman to proletarians, or eliminated them altogether, forcing them to move to urban areas to work in a factory. Thus, the new market revolution sucked the life out of the peasant village.[10]

The issue of slavery could not have been the sole factor that set in motion the events of the Civil War if less than 5 percent of Southern whites owned slaves, as some estimates claim.[11] An agrarian way of life that was threatened by the Industrial Revolution was also a major factor.[12] An agrarian is someone who identifies with a spot of ground, wrote John Crowe Ransom in *I'll Take My Stand*. A person finds it natural to think upon, explore, respect, and love a spot of ground, and one cannot do this with a "turn over" or a "natural resource" or "pile of money."[13] In the humble opinion of the Fugitive-Agrarians—and it was a humble opinion—industrialism dehumanized life.

The "Southern tradition" was actually the "English tradition" before the economic tumults of the eighteenth and nineteenth centuries swept them both away. The principal question the twelve Southerners were addressing centered on whether the South would permit the new economic order completely to eradicate its customs, landscape, and philosophy of life. These arts included dress, conversation, manners, the table, the hunt, politics, oratory, and the pulpit.[14] These were not the arts of escape, says Ransom, but of living; they were also arts the entire community could enjoy, not just one particular class. The Fugitive-Agrarians saw empty promises in the rhetoric of progress. What they feared was societal deformity brought on by a vicious cycle of material pursuit. Industrialism brutalized and hurried nature's design. It transformed cities into large artificial habitations, giving a false sense of exercising power over the natural world; nature would become lost in artificiality; all mystery would be drained out of it. If everyone became a consumer, then the notions of vocation and leisure

10. Ibid., 57–58.

11. Franklin and Moss, *From Slavery to Freedom*, 123.

12. See Owsley, "Irrepressible Conflict," 87.

13. Ransom, "Reconstructed but Unregenerate," 19–20.

14. Ibid., 12.

would have to be redefined. Religion would have to be redefined as well, because sacredness is determined by a correct view of nature.

The Tennessee town in which I was born now marks its city limits with signs that read: Clarksville, Gateway to the New South. If by this, city planners mean "free of racial prejudice," then I am happy for it. But I think the planners are saying something else. What I think they mean by "New South" is non-agrarian, corporate-friendly, and economically progressive. Like so many Southern towns, Clarksville's farm-based economy slipped away just after World War II, never to return. Although I am glad Southerners remain a friendly, well-mannered lot, what the Fugitive-Agrarians warned us about has come to pass. Industrialism and its successor, globalism, has rolled over us.

During the summer of 2006 my wife and I made a road trip from Clarksville to Pensacola for my daughter's wedding. Joining us was my oldest sister, who allowed us to pack the bed of her pickup truck with my daughter's belongings. Several years previously, my sister made what she considered to be a rational decision never to drive on the interstate system again, believing there were now too many eighteen-wheelers on these roads, and the chances of getting crushed to death by one of them was statistically probable, especially if under an inevitable panic attack. So we determined to take the local highways and enjoy the countryside, even if what was normally an eight-hour trip ended up lasting fourteen hours.

We were pleased to find some expected beautiful interludes of scenery spread out between the towns and traffic lights, but I was disappointed when traveling through the city of Huntsville, Alabama, a place I had visited some forty years before as a child. We should have taken the interstate. I have been told there are attractive places in Huntsville, but I did not see any. What I saw was miles of asphalt, billboards, box buildings, business signs, cars, communication towers, convenience stores, electric wires, gas stations, McDonald's golden arches, metal buildings, overpasses, Pizza Huts, telephone poles, traffic lights, traffic signs, traffic, trucks, underpasses, and Walmarts. It was as if the city planners of Huntsville had sat down and asked themselves, "O.K., how ugly can we make this place?"

In the past a community was considered to be an embodiment of its values. What, then, does our current landscape suggest about our belief system? We cannot love or care about places that possess so little beauty. Tolkien described Mordor as a vast wasteland: "Here nothing lived, not even the leprous growths that feed on rottenness. The gasping pools were choked with ash and crawling muds, sickly white and grey, as if the mountains had vomited the filth of their entrails upon the lands about."[15] The subtext of the *Ring* trilogy is obviously about the violation of the earth, and the culmination of the story is the scouring of the Shire. When the hobbits return from their quest, they find the Shire ravished by the Sharkeys of the world: "'This is worse than Mordor!' said Sam. 'Much worse in a way. It comes home to you, as they say; because it is home, and you remember it before it was all ruined.'"[16]

When this band of brothers returned to the Shire, they were shocked by what they saw—thugs running things, smokestacks, displaced hobbits, ruined gardens, and ugly houses. The veterans of Mordor immediately rolled up their sleeves and went to work restoring their community.

When the Greatest Generation returned from the European and Pacific theaters, they also rolled up their sleeves. But unlike Sam and company, the veterans of World War II applied their newfound courage and skills to erecting bigger factories, displacing more people, and building an even more powerful economic dynamo of mass consumption. The assembly lines of guns, tanks, and planes were simply replaced with assembly lines of cars, dishwashers, and television sets. There was nothing malicious about ratcheting up the economy a notch or two. The goal was to make our lives more comfortable. After all, this was progress.

And what American wants to argue with progress? Perhaps a better question would be, what American *can* argue with progress? The fly in the ointment of classical economic theory is moral neutrality, which prevents us from questioning its excesses. Actually, classical economics is not totally neutral because it favors utilitarian individualism, as Tocqueville quickly perceived. So, it is just understood by everyone that you do not question the values of bigger, faster, and more.

The era of Reagan represented a mind-split. On one hand, it was determined that laissez-faire economics should have its sovereign way, and, on the other hand, it was determined that something should be done to win back what was lost during the tumultuous Sixties and Seventies. But few adherents of the Moral Majority ever stopped to consider how the first front (unbridled consumerism) squelched the second one (traditional morality).

Ann Coulter once blurted out, "God gave us the earth. We have dominion over the plants, the animals, trees. God said, 'Earth is yours. Take it.

15. Tolkien, *Two Towers*, 617.
16. Tolkien, *Return of the King*, 994.

Rape it. It's yours.'"[17] Tolkien would have been repulsed by such an assertion. What is odd is that the sentiment originated from a political "conservative." Coulter fails to see any incompatibility between unbridled consumerism and traditional morality. For this reason, her outlook is thoroughly liberal rather than conservative. Radical individualism is now established doctrine for both political parties. Democrats do not want anyone limiting the use of their genitals; Republicans do not want anyone limiting the use of their wallets. Self-restraint, community building, and passing on a heritage to our children get little play on either side of the political aisle.

Bigger and *faster* and *more* are insufficient values upon which to build a community. And yet these are the major tenets of technological society. There exists an older, deeper conservatism that has already forcefully criticized modernity. One of our best tools to evaluate technological society comes from the Christian humanist tradition. Progressive liberals should heed the warning of C. S. Lewis's *The Abolition of Man* that the conquest of nature could easily become nature's conquest of man: that when the old task of transferring wisdom from one generation to the other ceases—only to be replaced by a manipulation of humanity by those who have the raw power to do it—the purpose of man has been abandoned.[18]

T. S. Eliot was essentially making the same warning in *The Waste Land*. His poem looks to the past and not the future for solutions to modernity's bareness. The poet was saying, "Nothing holy can exist here. Civilization is not progressing; to the contrary, it is sliding."

In the *Waste Land* we see desolation:

What are the roots that clutch, what branches grow
Out of this stony rubbish? (ll. 19–20)

Futility:

"What is that noise now? What is the wind doing?"
Nothing again nothing. (ll. 119–20)

Despair:

I see crowds of people, walking round in a ring. (l. 56)

Tolkien was making the same warning. Technological society is the black fist jutting up from the hollowed plain of Isengard where no green thing grows. It is Mordor, that "vast fortress, armoury, prison, furnace of great power . . . which suffered no rival, and laughed at flattery, biding its time, secure in its pride and immeasurable strength."

17. *Washington Monthly*, "Wisdom of Ann Coulter," para. 6.
18. See Lewis, *Abolition of Man*, 87–88.

Tolkien was appalled at industrialism, but now industrialism has taken on a red hue as we slide into what Marshall McLuhan called a universal consciousness where everybody is connected to everybody. Some celebrate this interconnectedness; others exploit it for profit. When Thomas Friedman says in *The World Is Flat*, "If it can be digitized, it can be outsourced,"[19] I am reminded of Wendell Berry's quip: "Global thinkers have been and will be dangerous people."[20] Friedman is a celebrant of change and this is why he tells his readers that a flat world is "inevitable and unavoidable."[21] Is this not the voice of the Dark Lord?

In a 2004 interview with *Newsweek*, Sergey Brin, cofounder of Google, remarked, "Certainly if you had all the world's information directly attached to your brain, or an artificial brain, you'd be better off."[22] Brin's comment is not unlike the cold line of The Borg of *Star Trek* fame, blurted just before it puts your brain in an electronic vise-grip: *Resistance is futile.* The Borg cube comes at you at Warp 10 speed, hell-bent on sticking a nanoprobe under your skin, rewriting your DNA, and transforming your organs into machine parts. They are not interested in a truce. They will not smoke the peace pipe. They will not be happy (if they can be happy) until you and everybody else has been assimilated. And once that is done, once the silicon tube is jutting out of your neck into your new skull mask, you have not only lost your soul, but you are working for them. "They took everything I was," Picard tells his brother after being borged, "They used me to kill and to destroy and I couldn't stop them." When one of the founders of Google says we would be better off if the entire world's information was attached directly to our brains, then you know, the times they are a changin'.

Back to the Shire

I am not so naive as to suggest that we can recapture an idyllic agrarian past. For one thing, I am not sure an idyllic agrarian past ever existed, even in Bag End. Pre-industrial villages were not misery-free. Back-breaking toil, early death, and the plague could be found in Old World communities.

---

19. Friedman, *World Is Flat*, 15. To Friedman's credit it should be noted that he has recently restrained his optimism about a flat world, calling for America to lead in a "green revolution" in his new book *Hot, Flat, and Crowded*.

20. Berry, "Out of Your Car, Off Your Horse," 19.

21. Friedman, *World Is Flat*, 49.

22. Quoted in Carr, "Is Google Making Us Stupid?" 63.

What agrarians and New Urbanists want are alternatives to the depressing monoculture that is now wrapping its tentacles around the globe. Our current economic crisis should make us pause and ask if there is something inherently wrong with the excesses associated with modern capitalism. There has got to be a better way.

One might think that agrarians would be suspicious of the word "urban." But both movements share a disdain for what is bland, artificial, and hideous. Both movements are deliberate in their attempts to resist the Machine and, conversely, to create something more organic, sustainable, and livable. Agrarians and New Urbanists understand that there is a correlation between what a culture makes and what that culture becomes—this is a spiritual truth for them. A more beautiful and livable infrastructure is not the cure-all for spiritual impoverishment, but ugly human creations are certainly a symptom of it, and building better places to live is one important part of restoring family, church, and community. These institutions are not thriving now, and I doubt if they could thrive in a *Matrix*-like existence, which is where technological society seems to be heading.

So imagine, if you will, a very small town (a polis of about 1,000 people), as opposed to what used to be a neighborhood, where you walk to church, school, and the grocery store. Only, it is not called a grocery store, but a community market with locally grown foodstuffs. (The polis is not zoned for Walmart or McDonald's.) The items in the market were not raised on an industrial farm two thousand miles away, or overseas, but on a family farm or the Commons close to where you live. What you call the "city" is twenty-five miles as the crow flies, and urbanites take the rail on weekends to hike, bike, fish, or purchase produce at the market. Your husband takes the same rail to work two days a week. You have solar panels on the roof and a wood-burning stove next to the kitchen. The stove is heated by timber fuel harvested on a hillside within the Commons. When you look out the window you can see your oldest child milking Betsy. He wants to work at the Commons this summer with his friends. "Everybody's doing it," he says. The middle child is building a tree house in the apple orchard with the kid next door. The youngest is trying to catch a chicken in the backyard. The dog is barking. Not all the neighbors have as many animals, but every year some new species seems to get added to the eight-acre spread. Your husband walks through the backdoor with a cut of roses in one hand and a bucket of asparagus in the other. You stop him at the threshold. "Why don't we take the kids to Hub Hall tonight? Cousin Thaddeus is playing in the

Bluegrass band, and I hear they're really good." Grandma, who is standing at the stove stirring a pot of soup, turns her head and says, "I want to go too!" For someone who is 102, she still has lots of energy.

We might call this a new agrarian vision for the twenty-first century, and maybe centuries to come. Idyllic? Somewhat. Attainable? Perhaps. Needed? Absolutely. The Shire represents permanence, a sense of place, and harmony with nature. Mordor is endless and reckless growth in the name of "progress." The agrarian vision is more than nostalgic longing; it is the antidote to what ails the earth, and to some extent what ails our souls. The antithesis to this vision is George Jetson rotating round and round on his treadmill outside the Skypad Apartments shouting, "Jane, stop this crazy thing!"

Returning to the Shire is a necessity for three reasons. First, our current way of doing agriculture is vulnerable to acts of terrorism. For that matter, any far flung, fossil-fuel dependent economy is vulnerable. Localized economies are less so, which is why the best Home Land Security begins with the *home* and its immediate surroundings. Second, Mordor is not sustainable. It will eventually collapse upon itself. The possibility of an ecological meltdown is real. We are past the time when an economist can make a forecast and not consider soil erosion, water and air pollution, deforestation, and global warming. Third, the materialist paradigm of consumerism is spiritually impoverished. Most of us are oblivious to this malady, but we cannot deny our increased sense of unhappiness and despair, what Søren Kierkegaard referred to as a feeling of dread, of being utterly overwhelmed.

As to the attainability of the new agrarian vision, several obstacles are standing in its way. First among these are the large corporations. The question really boils down to this: Who is going to have control over the land? Will it be the giant psychopaths who have shown a pattern of abuse and disdain for local things, or will it be men and women who naturally care for the land because they live on it, work it, and love it? We need legal incentives that would allow for the resettling of farm land by many owners and users, not just the few. To go one step further, there needs to be a constitutional presumption that favors families, communities, and local regions over the corporation, a condition that might only be achieved through stripping corporations of their "real person" status. Economic policies that favor large-scale production, long-distance distribution, and environmental-wrecking practices need to be reversed so that *small* once again becomes a beautiful word. E. F. Schumacher eloquently contended that what we need is an economic framework designed for small business and the little person.[23]

Being green is now fashionable, and there seems to be a promising conversation about eco-friendly technologies. The new agrarian vision is not anti-technology. Such a stance is the equivalent of being, as Neil Postman put it, anti-food.[24] All technologies are extensions of our bodies, and therefore appropriate scale and ecological impact becomes the yardstick of technological wisdom. The use of energy-efficient, renewable, decentralized, technologies like solar and wind power become the standard within the new agrarian vision.

A major obstacle that prevents us from returning to the Shire is the doctrine of inevitability, which says you cannot go back; you cannot stop progress. We must answer that life would not be worthwhile if we have no choice in the matter. If we say it cannot be done, if we corner ourselves into impotence, then it *is* all over. Man has been abolished, and the shadow of Mordor has prevailed.

Finally, a return to the Shire is futile if a deliberate sacramentalism does not accompany it. Such a sacramentalism must include an understanding of what people are for and the recognition of a divine moral order. A healthy metaphysic that acknowledges words like "sin" and "greed" and "idolatry" serves to restrain utilitarian individualism run afoul.

The remarkable virtues of Frodo and Sam are courage and fortitude, and these are the virtues needed to take back the Shire. But we must imagine it first and see the necessity of it. The odds are daunting, the hour is late, but the stakes are too high to do nothing.

23. See Schumacher, *Small Is Beautiful.*

24. Postman, *Building a Bridge to the Eighteenth Century*, 44.

Permissions and Credits

A MUCH BRIEFER VERSION of "Remembering Marshall McLuhan: The Probes of the Media Guru Are Still Relevant for Us Today" appeared as "Marshall McLuhan: What Were You Doin'? Coiner of 'The Global Village' Turns One Hundred" in *The Christian Research Journal* 34/6 (2011).

A similar version of "Neil Postman and the Evangelicals" appeared in *EME: Exploration in Media Ecology: The Journal of the Media Ecology Association* 5/1 (2007). It was also presented at a symposium at New York University honoring the life and work of Neil Postman, April 6, 2006. A similar version also appeared in *Second Nature*, an online journal for critical thinking about technology and new media in the light of the Christian tradition, under the title, "The Secular C. S. Lewis: Neil Postman's Unlikely Influence on Evangelicals," (May, 2013). Online: http://www.secondnature-journal.com/author/arthur-hunt/.

"The Image Versus the Word: Old Story, New Twist: A Lament from a Christian Media Ecologist" received the Top Academic Paper Award at the Fourth Annual Media Ecology Association Convention in 2003. For an amplified version of this essay see my book, *The Vanishing Word: The Veneration of Visual Imagery in the Postmodern World*. Wheaton, IL: Crossway Books, 2003.

A similar version of "Why I Am Not Going to Teach Public Speaking Online," appeared in *EME: Exploration in Media Ecology: The Journal of the Media Ecology Association* 11/2 (2013). It was also presented as a paper at the Fourteenth Annual Convention of the Media Ecology Association, 2013, at Grand Valley State University in Grand Rapids, Michigan.

A similar version of "Progress: What Happens When We Get Too Big for Our Britches," was presented at the Stephen Olford Center at Union University, Memphis, Tennessee, as a part of the 2013 Christianity in the Academy Conference, "C. S. Lewis, 50 Years On: What Endures?"

Permissions and Credits

"What's a Person to Do? Work Beyond the Yellow Brick Road" was presented at Union University, Jackson, Tennessee, as a part of the 2011 Town & Gown Series on Technology and Culture.

A shorter version of "Oikos: A Case for Reviving Household Economy" appeared in *Reformation21*, The Online Magazine of the Alliance of Confessing Evangelicals (January 2012). Online: http://www.reformation21. org/articles/oikos-a-case-for-reviving-the-household-economy.php.

"Back to the Shire: From English Village, to Global Village, and Back Again" appeared in *Modern Age* 51/3&4 (2009). It was presented at a 2010 forum sponsored by the College of Humanities and Fine Arts at the University of Tennessee in Martin. It was also presented at Union University, Jackson Tennessee, as a part of the 2011 Town & Gown Series on Technology and Culture.

All previously published material is used here by permission of the aforementioned original publishers.

Bibliography

Alliance of Confessing Evangelicals. "The Cambridge Declaration." April 20, 1996. No pages. Online: http://www.alliancenet.org/partner/Article_Display_Page/0,, PTID307086_CHID615424_CIID1411364,00.html.

Bakan, Joel. *The Corporation: The Pathological Pursuit of Profit and Power*. New York: Free Press, 2005.

———. "The Kids Are Not All Right." *New York Times*, August 21, 2011. No pages. Online: http://www.nytimes.com/2011/08/22/opinion/corporate-interests-threaten-chil drens-welfare.html?_r=1.

Barber, Benjamin R. *Consumed: How Markets Corrupt Children, Infantilize Adults, and Swallow Citizens Whole*. New York: Norton, 2007.

———. *Jihad vs. McWorld: Terrorism's Challenge to Democracy*. New York: Ballantine, 1995.

Berry, Wendell. "Feminism, the Body, and the Machine." In *What Are People For? Essays*, 178–96. New York: North Point, 1990.

———. "Out of Your Car, Off Your Horse." In *Sex, Economy, Freedom & Community: Eight Essays*, 19–26. New York: Pantheon, 1993.

———. "Stupidity in Concentration." In *Bringing It to the Table: On Farming and Food*, 11–18. Berkeley, CA: Counterpoint, 2009.

———. *The Unsettling of America: Culture and Agriculture*. San Francisco: Sierra Club, 1997.

———. "The Whole Horse." In *Citizenship Papers: Essays*, 113–26. Washington, DC: Shoemaker & Hoard, 2002.

———. "Why I Am Not Going to Buy a Computer." In *What Are People For?*, 170–77. New York: North Point, 1990.

Binder, Alan S. "Offshoring: The Next Industrial Revolution?" *Foreign Affairs* 85 (2006) 113–28.

Boardman, John, et al., editors. *The Oxford History of the Classical World*. New York: Oxford University Press, 1986.

Boorstin, Daniel. *The Image: A Guide to Pseudo-Events in America*. 1961. Reprint, New York: Vintage, 1987.

Bremer, Francis J. *The Puritan Experiment: New England Society from Bradford to Edwards*. New York: St. Martin's, 1976.

Bury, John B. *The Idea of Progress: An Inquiry into its Origin and Growth*. New York: Dover, 1955.

Bibliography

Bushman, Richard L. *From Puritan to Yankee: Character and the Social Order in Connecticut, 1690–1765.* Cambridge: Harvard University Press, 1967.

Carlson, Allan C., and Paul T. Mero. "A Natural Family Policy." In *The Natural Family: A Manifesto*, 189–207. Dallas: Spence, 2007.

Carpenter, Humphrey. *Tolkien: A Biography*. Boston: Houghton Mifflin, 1977.

Carr, Nicholas. "Is Google Making Us Stupid? What the Internet Is Doing to Our Brains." *Atlantic Monthly*, July/August 2008.

Carson, D. A. *Christ & Culture Revisited*. Grand Rapids: Eerdmans, 2008.

Chesterton, G. K. "The Emancipation of Domesticity" In *What's Wrong with the World*, 126–34. 1910. Reprint, New York: Simon & Brown, 2011.

Christensen, Bryce. "Divided We Fall: America's Second Civil War." Howard Center for Family, Religion, and Society. No pages. Online: http://www.profam.org/pub/fia/fia_1710.htm?search=divorce rate&opt=EXACT#fn44.

Christians, Clifford G. "Ellul as Theologian In Counterpoint." In *Perspectives on Culture, Technology and Communication: The Media Ecology Tradition*, edited by Casey Man Kong Lum, 117–41. Cresskill, NJ: Hampton, 2006.

Cowan, Ruth Schwartz. *More Work for Mother: The Ironies of Household Technology from the Open Hearth to the Microwave*. New York: Basic Books, 1983.

Crawford, Matthew B. *Shop Class as Soulcraft: An Inquiry into the Value of Work*. New York: Penguin, 2009.

Crouch, Andy. *Culture Making: Recovering Our Creative Calling*. Downers Grove, IL: IVP, 2008.

Czitrom, Daniel J. *Media and the American Mind: From Morse to McLuhan*. Chapel Hill: University of North Carolina Press, 1982.

Davies, Lorraine, et al. "Significant Life Experiences and Depression Among Single and Married Mothers." *Journal of Marriage and the Family* 59 (1997) 294–308.

Dawn, Marva J. *Reaching Out Without Dumbing Down: A Theology of Worship for the Turn-of-the-Century Culture*. Grand Rapids: Eerdmans, 1995.

Dernbach, C. "In Focus: WTO and Sustainable Development." Published as part of "Foreign Policy in Focus," a joint project of the Interhemispheric Resource Center and the Institute for Policy Studies. No pages. Online: www.foreignpolicy-infocus.org.

Dreher, Rod. "A Crunchy Con Manifesto." In *Crunchy Cons*, 1–2. New York: Crown Forum, 2006.

Durant, Will. *The Reformation: A History of European Civilization from Wycliffe to Calvin: 1300–1564*. New York: MJF, 1992.

Eisenstein, Elizabeth L. *The Printing Revolution in Early Modern Europe*. New York: Cambridge University Press, 1983.

Eliot, T. S. *The Idea of a Christian Society*. London: Faber & Faber, 1939.

Ellul, Jacques. *The Presence of the Kingdom*. Translated by Olive Wyon. 1948. Reprint, New York: Seabury, 1967.

———. *Propaganda: The Formation of Men's Attitudes*. Translated by Konrad Kellen and Jean Lerner. 1965. Reprint, New York: Knopf, 1968.

———. *The Technological Bluff*. Translated by Geoffrey W. Bromiley. Grand Rapids: Eerdmans, 1990.

———. *The Technological Society*. Translated by Robert K. Merton. 1964. Reprint, New York: Knopf, 1967.

Ewen, Stuart. *All Consuming Images: The Politics of Style in Contemporary Culture.* New York: Basic Books, 1988.

Ffinch, Michael. *G. K. Chesterton.* Cambridge: Harper & Row, 1986.

Flammang, Janet A. *The Taste for Civilization: Food, Politics, and Civil Society.* Urbana: University of Illinois Press, 2009.

Fletcher, John Gould. "Education, Past and Present." In *I'll Take My Stand: The South and the Agrarian Tradition,* edited by Lewis P. Simpson, 92–121. 1930. Reprint, Baton Rouge: Louisiana State University, 1980.

Franklin, John Hope, and Alfred A. Moss Jr. *From Slavery to Freedom.* 7th ed. New York: McGraw-Hill, 1994.

Friedman, Thomas L. *The World Is Flat: A Brief History of the Twenty-First Century: Updated and Expanded.* New York: Farrar, Straus & Giroux, 2006.

Gelernter, David. *1939: The Lost World of the Fair.* New York: Free Press, 1995.

Gencarelli, Tom. "The Intellectual Roots of Media Ecology in the Work and Thought of Neil Postman." *New Jersey Journal of Communication* 8 (2000) 91–103.

Godfrey, W. Robert. "Experiencing a Congregation, Psalm 84." In *An Unexpected Journey: Discovering Reformed Christianity,* 23–30. Phillipsburg, NJ: P&R, 2004.

Goldstein, Norm. *The History of Television.* New York: Portland House, 1991.

Gordon, T. David. "Neil Postman (1931–2003): Some Recollections." *PRESSthink: Ghost of Democracy in the Media Machine,* a blog by Jay Rosen, October 7, 2003. No pages. Online: http://archive.pressthink.org/2003/10/07/postman_life.html.

———. *Why Johnny Can't Preach: The Media Have Shaped the Messengers.* Phillipsburg, NJ: P. & R., 2009.

Gordon, W. Terrence. *Marshall McLuhan: Escape into Understanding: A Biography.* New York: Basic, 1997.

Guinness, Os. *Fit Bodies, Fat Minds: Why Evangelicals Don't Think and What to Do about It.* Grand Rapids: Baker, 1994.

Hart, D. G. "Wendell Berry's Unlikely Case for Conservative Christianity." In *The Humane Vision of Wendell Berry,* edited by Mark T. Mitchell and Nathan Schuleter, 124–46. Wilmington, DE: ISI, 2011.

Highet, Gilbert. *The Art of Teaching.* 1950. Reprint, New York: Vintage, 1989.

Holmes, Oliver Wendell. "The Stereoscope and the Stereograph." *Atlantic Monthly,* June 1859. Reprinted in *Photography Essays and Images,* edited by Beaumont Newhall, 53–54. New York: Museum of Modern Art, 1980.

Hong, Gong-Soong, and Shelley I. White-Means. "Do Working Mothers Have Healthy Children?" *Journal of Family and Economic Issues* 14 (1993) 163–81.

Jardine, Murray. *The Making and Unmaking of Technological Society: How Christianity Can Save Modernity from Itself.* Grand Rapids: Brazos, 2004.

Köstenberger, Andreas J. *God, Marriage, and Family: Rebuilding the Biblical Foundation.* Wheaton, IL: Crossway, 2004.

Lanier, Lyle H. "A Critique of the Philosophy of Progress." In *I'll Take My Stand: The South and the Agrarian Tradition,* edited by Lewis P. Simpson, 122–54. 1930. Reprint, Baton Rouge: Louisiana State University, 1980.

Lasch, Christopher. *The Culture of Narcissism: American Life in an Age of Diminishing Expectations.* New York: Warner, 1979.

Laslet, Peter. *The World We Have Lost.* New York: Scribner's, 1966.

Leonard, Annie. "Story of Stuff, Referenced and Annotated Script." StoryOfStuff.com, 1–16. Online: http://dev.storyofstuff.org/wp-content/uploads/2011/10/annie_leonard_footnoted_script.pdf.

Lewis, C. S. *The Abolition of Man.* 1947. Reprint, New York: Macmillian, 1968.

———. *Mere Christianity.* 1952. Reprint, New York: HarperSanFrancisco, 1980.

Liptak, Adam. "1 in 100 U.S. Adults Behind Bars, New Study Says." *New York Times,* February 28, 2008. No pages. Online: http://www.nytimes.com/2008/02/28/us/28cnd-prison.html?_r=3&hp&oref=slogin&oref=slogin.

Lockridge, Kenneth A. *A New England Town: The First Hundred Years.* Enl. ed. New York: Norton, 1985.

MacMullen, Ramsay. *Christianity & Paganism in the Fourth to Eighth Centuries.* New Haven: Yale University Press, 1997.

Manchester, William. *A World Lit Only by Fire: The Medieval Mind and the Renaissance.* Boston: Little, Brown, 1992.

Marchand, Philip. *Marshall McLuhan: The Medium and the Messenger.* Cambridge: MIT Press, 1998.

Marsden, George. *Jonathan Edwards: A Life.* New Haven: Yale University Press, 2003.

McLuhan, Eric, and Frank Zingrone, editors. *Essential McLuhan.* New York: Basic Books, 1995.

McLuhan, Marshall. *The Gutenberg Galaxy: The Making of Typographic Man.* Toronto: University of Toronto Press, 1962.

———. *The Medium Is the Massage: An Inventory of Effects.* New York: Bantam, 1967.

———. "Southern Quality." *Sewanee Review* 55 (1947) 357–83.

Médaille, John C. *Toward a Truly Free Market: A Distributist Perspective on the Role of Government, Taxes, Health Care, Deficits, and More.* Wilmington, DE: ISI, 2010.

Merskey, Helen S., and G. T. Swart. "Family Background and Physical Health of Adolescents Admitted to an Inpatient Psychiatric Unit." *Canadian Journal of Psychiatry* 34 (1989) 79–83.

Metaxas, Eric. *Bonhoeffer: Pastor, Martyr, Prophet, Spy.* Nashville: Thomas Nelson, 2010.

Meyrowitz, Joshua. "Canonic Anti-Text: Marshall McLuhan's *Understanding Media.*" In *Canonic Texts in Media Research: Are There Any? Should There Be? How About These?,* edited by Elihu Katz et al., 191–52. Cambridge, MA: Polity, 2003.

Millard, Alan R. "The Practice of Writing in Ancient Israel." *Biblical Archaeologist* 4 (1972) 98–111.

———. "The Question of Israelite Literacy." *Bible Review* 3 (1987) 22–31.

Miller, Eric. *Hope in a Scattering Time: A Life of Christopher Lasch.* Grand Rapids: Eerdmans, 2010.

Molinaro, Matie, et al., editors. *Letters of Marshall McLuhan.* New York: Oxford University Press, 1987.

Monke, Lowell. "Charlette's Webpage: Why Children Shouldn't Have the World at Their Fingertips." *Orion* 24 (2005) 25–31.

Murray, Iain. *Jonathan Edwards: A New Biography.* Carlisle, PA: Banner of Truth Trust, 1987.

Myers, Kenneth. *All God's Children and Blue Suede Shoes: Christians & Popular Culture.* Westchester, IL: Crossway, 1989.

Noll, Mark. *American Evangelicalism: An Introduction.* Oxford: Blackwell, 2001.

Ong, Walter J. *Orality and Literacy: The Technologizing of the Word.* 1982. Reprint, New York: Routledge, 2002.

Owsley, Frank Lawrence. "The Irrepressible Conflict." In *I'll Take My Stand: The South and the Agrarian Tradition*, edited by Lewis P. Simpson, 61–91. 1930. Reprint, Baton Rouge: Louisiana State University, 1980.

Paglia, Camille. *Sexual Personae: Art and Decadence from Nefertiti to Emily Dickinson.* London: Yale University Press, 1990.

Pearce, Joseph. *Small Is Still Beautiful: Economics as if Families Mattered.* Wilmington, DE: ISI, 2006.

Popenoe, David, and Barbara Dafoe Whitehead. "Should We Live Together? What Young Adults Need to Know about Cohabitation Before Marriage." National Marriage Project. 2010. No pages. Online: http://www.smartmarriages.com/cohabit.html.

Postman, Neil. *Amusing Ourselves to Death: Public Discourse in the Age of Show Business.* New York: Penguin, 1985.

———. *Building a Bridge to the Eighteenth Century: How the Past Can Improve Our Future.* New York: Knofp, 1999.

———. *The Disappearance of Childhood.* New York: Vintage, 1992.

———. *The End of Education: Redefining the Value of School.* New York: Vintage, 1995.

———. Foreword to *Marshall McLuhan: The Medium and the Messenger*, by Philip Marchand, vii-xiii. Cambridge: MIT Press, 1998.

———. "The Humanism of Media Ecology." *Proceedings of the Media Ecology Association* 1 (2000) no pages. Online: http://www.media-ecology.org/publications/MEA_proceedings/v1/index.html.

———. "Science and the Story that We Need." *First Things* 69 (1997) 29–32.

———. *Teaching as a Conserving Activity.* New York: Delacorte, 1979.

———. "What Is Media Ecology?" Media Ecology Association. No pages. Online: http://www.media-ecology.org/media_ecology/.

Postman, Neil, and Camille Paglia. "She Wants Her TV! He Wants His Book!" *Harpers*, March 1991.

Ransom, David. "Globalization on the Rocks." *New Internationalist*, March 2010. Online: http://newint.org/features/2010/03/01/keynote-globalization/.

Ransom, John Crowe. "Reconstructed but Unregenerate." In *I'll Take My Stand: The South and the Agrarian Tradition*, edited by Lewis P. Simpson, 1–27. 1930. Reprint, Baton Rouge: Louisiana State University, 1980.

Reynolds, Gregory. *The Word Is Worth a Thousand Pictures: Preaching in the Electronic Age.* Eugene, OR: Wipf & Stock, 2001.

Robinson, Marilynne. "Darwinism." In *The Death of Adam: Essays on Modern Thought*, 28–75. 1998. Reprint, New York: Picador, 2005.

———. *When I Was a Child I Read Books.* New York: Farrar, Straus & Giroux, 2012.

Rosin, Hanna. "The End of Men: How Women Are Taking Control—of Everything." *Atlantic Monthly*, July/August 2010.

Sale, Kirkpatrick. Foreword to *Beyond Capitalism & Socialism: A New Statement of an Old Ideal*, edited by Tobias J. Lanz, xi-xii. Norfolk, VA: IHS, 2008.

Schumacher, E. F. *Small Is Beautiful: Economics as if People Mattered: 25 Years Later.* Point Roberts, WA: Hartley & Marks, 1999.

Slouka, Mark. *War of the Worlds: Cyberspace and the High-Tech Assault on Reality.* New York: Basic Books, 1995.

Tolkien, J. R. R. *The Return of the King.* 1955. Reprint, New York: Houghton Mifflin, 1994.

———. *The Two Towers.* 1954. Reprint, New York: Houghton Mifflin, 1994.

Tolson, Jay. "The New Old-Time Religion." *U.S. News & World Report*, December 8, 2003.

Bibliography

Townsend, Colin R., et al. *Essentials of Ecology.* 3rd ed. Malden, MA: Wiley-Blackwell, 2008.

Trueman, Carl. "Weber Again." *Reformation 21,* November 21, 2006. Online: http://www. reformation21.org/blog/2006/11/weber-again.php.

U.S. Bureau of the Census. "America's Families and Living Arrangements: 2003." Online: http://www.census.gov/prod/2004pubs/p20-553.pdf.

U.S. Department of Labor. Bureau of Labor Statistics. "Unemployment Rises Slightly to 9.0%." National Conference of State Legislatures, May 6, 2011. No pages. Online: http://www.ncsl.org/?tabid=13307.

USA Today. "Incomes of Young in 8-Year Nose Dive: Those Older than 54 Increase Earnings." September 18, 2009, A1.

Veith, Gene E. *Modern Fascism: Liquidating the Judeo-Christian Worldview.* St. Louis: Concordia, 1993.

———. *Postmodern Times: A Christian Guide to Contemporary Thought and Culture.* Wheaton, IL: Crossway, 1994.

———. *Reading Between the Lines: A Christian Guide to Literature.* Wheaton, IL: Crossway, 1990.

Ventura, Stephanie. "Changing Patterns of Nonmarital Childbearing in the United States." National Center for Health Statistics, May 2009. Online: http://www.cdc.gov/nchs/ data/databriefs/db18.pdf.

Washington Monthly. "The Wisdom of Ann Coulter." October 2001. Online: http://www. washingtonmonthly.com/features/2001/0111.coulterwisdom.html.

Weaver, Richard M. "Humanism in an Age of Science." In *In Defense of Tradition: Collected Shorter Writings of Richard M. Weaver, 1929–1963,* edited by Ted J. Smith, 61–72. Indianapolis: Liberty Fund, 2001.

———. *Ideas Have Consequences.* 1948. Reprint, Chicago: University of Chicago Press, 1984.

———. "Two Diarists." In *In Defense of Tradition,* 720–48. Indianapolis, IN: Liberty Fund, 2001.

Weber, Max. *The Protestant Ethic and the Spirit of Capitalism.* Translated by Talcott Parsons. 1930. Reprint, New York: Scribner's, 1958.

Wells, David F. Introduction to *The Compromised Church: The Present Evangelical Crisis,* edited by John H. Armstrong, 19–34. Wheaton, IL: Crossway, 1998.

Weyrich, Paul. "The Next Conservative Economics." *World,* August 5, 2005. Online: http://www.worldmag.com/webextra/11420.

White, E. B. "Removal." In *One Man's Meat,* 2–3. New York: Harper & Row, 1983.

Wilson, Douglass. "Educating the Imagination." In *The Case for Classical Christian Education,* 153–62. Wheaton, IL: Crossway, 2003.

Wilson, James R., and S. Roy Wilson. *Mass Media, Mass Culture: An Introduction.* 5th ed. New York: McGraw-Hill, 2001.

Wood, David. "Prime Time: Albert Borgmann on Taming Technology." *Christian Century* 120 (2003) 22.